STEVE ALLEN

KINGDOM TREASURES FROM THE LIFE OF ELIJAH
*AND MY PERSONAL **BATTLE WITH ALS***

AND HE

RAN

FOR 40 DAYS

A 40 DAY DEVOTIONAL JOURNAL

ANITA —   10-25-20

PURSUE HIM AS HE
PURSUES YOU!
PSALM 119:32

STEVE

Allen Family Ministries
Colorado Springs, Colorado, USA
allenfamilyministries.org

And He Ran for 40 Days
Kingdom Treasures from the Life of Elijah and My Personal Battle with ALS
Copyright © 2019 by Steve Allen.

Printed in the United States of America

For information contact:
Steve Allen - support@allenfamilyministries.org
https://allenfamilyministries.org

Book and cover design by 4Tower.com

ISBN: 978-1-7338107-2-2 (softcover)
ISBN: 978-1-7338107-3-9 (e-book)

First Edition: 2019

10 9 8 7 6 5 4 3 2 1

SIDNEY NAY ALLEN
1933 - 2018

Veterinarian, missionary to South Korea for 16 years, lieutenant colonel in the U.S. Army, loving husband to his beautiful wife Jenetta for 58 years, elder in the church, father to Laura, David, and Stephen, who have followed their parents serving in missions and ministry for a combined total of 83 years. This book is dedicated to my father who taught me what it means to be a man of God, a loving husband, and a godly father. Thank you, Dad, for walking the talk. Thank you for leading our family well and leaving me an example to run in.

This scripture is dedicated to you:

"He has shown you, O man, what is good. And what does the Lord require of you? To act justly and to love mercy and walk humbly with your God." Micah 6:8 NIV 1984

Spring of 2004: Dad on Michael and Sherry Irvin's farm in Central Texas, with his two grandsons Michael and Kanaan who are now in full-time ministry serving as fourth generation missionaries.

PHOTOGRAPHY

In the pages of this 40-day journal are the stunning landscape photographs by Grahm Foster. Grahm is a multi-talented individual. A writer, teacher, mentor, discipler, wood craftsman, devoted husband, and loving father. He's also my friend.

These beautiful photographs that you're about to view display the incredible creative power of our Living God. They were shot in California, Colorado, Maine, and Hawaii.

Throughout the biblical narrative, the desert has always been a place where God met with the people of Israel and men and women of God.[1]

Elijah spent 40 days in the desert on a personal quest to rediscover his identity and meet face to face with Jehovah God. May these beautiful photographs from nature inspire you and ignite worship in you for our amazing Creator!

I want to encourage you to go to Grahm Foster's photography website and purchase some of his beautiful prints as gifts for birthdays, anniversary celebrations, and Christmas.

Steve Allen

www.grahmfoster.com

---

[1] From the teachings of Michael Niebur
Team Leader Derech Avraham
Jerusalem, Israel

This photograph was taken in 2011 from the top of Mauna Kea Volcano on The Big Island of Hawaii. It's a 14er. Amazing views. One of the clearest places on earth to see out of our atmosphere.

ACKNOWLEDGEMENTS

In the process of writing this devotional journal, it is quite apparent to me the power of synergy where the whole is greater than the sum of its parts. I am completely aware, humbled, and grateful that I am the fruit of many who have fathered, mentored, taught, trained, and poured into me.

I would like to thank:

All those who helped me in the final stages of this book with editing: Clint McDowell, Laura Allen, Michelle Allen, Jay Capra, Jon Pinkston, Grahm Foster, and my editor Tarrah Teigland who did a fabulous job!

A special thanks to my good friend Mauro Cavassana, who is the best brand manager in the industry! Thank you for the last 11 years of friendship. Your stellar work, with our websites, coaching material, and books has been exceptional. As usual, you went the extra mile in the layout, formatting, and publishing of this book. Thank you! Please check out Mauro's website: www.4tower.com

My best friend, Russ Pennington, who since college, has proven to be a friend who sticks closer than a brother. Thank you for 33 years of friendship. Thank you for being such a stellar model of a man who shares his faith everywhere he goes. You are one in a million! I love you Russ!

My mentor Clint McDowell, who has walked with me for the last 28 years. Thank you for your incredible steadfastness of a man of God who has spoken the Word of the Lord over my life multiple times.

David Fitzpatrick, a spiritual father whom the Lord sent to me in the summer of 2018, in a season of transition. Thank you for your wisdom and counsel. It was invaluable. Thank you for your continued friendship, wisdom, and mentoring.

My spiritual son Zach Garza, who is a prince of a man! You're changing the future destiny of hundreds of young men in inner city Dallas through Forerunner Mentoring. You're raising up your 100,000! I'm so proud of you! So grateful for the way that you've chosen to be a servant leader in His Kingdom.

A special thanks to our home church, Grace Center, in Franklin, Tennessee, with whom we worshiped the last 10 years. Thank you, Jeff and Becky Dollar, for creating an atmosphere for the presence of God to come and rest. Thank you to the Grace Center Mission Team whom we had the privilege of serving with for 8 years: Mike and Sisse Pfeiffer, Doug and Dabney Mann, Tony and Laura Wakefield, Ryan and Katie Robinson, Shelly Boer, and Tetra Cierpke. You all are amazing!

Heartfelt thanks to our Life Group in Nashville, Tennessee. It was a great honor and joy to walk together with you for the last 10 years. Thank you to the following amazing families: Pickmans, Glasels, Johnsons, d'Artenays, Cavassanas, McCrays, Kreiders, Marcuses, Ron Peterson, and Sue Roth.

I'm grateful for the Caleb Company family, board, and community. Thank you for 10 years of impacting and blessing my family and me. A special thanks to Papa Don Finto, Jon and Gerri Bridston, Tod and Rachel McDowell, and Ben and Emily DeBose. Thank you to the Caleb staff: Maury Weldon, Hunter Stewart, Judah and Mindi Robinson, Kendra Blalock, Heather Kalua, Jesse and Lauren Martin, and Megan Mandel. You are amazing!

Thank you to our faith community here in Colorado Springs: Chris and Susan Berglund, Paul and Cheryl Amabile, Grahm and Sarah Foster, and Nathan and Barbie Carr. A special thanks to Lou and Therese Engle for being leaders in this movement. You're the reason why we are here!

Thank you to Contend Global, the ministry that we have had the privilege of serving with this past year and a half. Thank you, David and Audry Kim, for being amazing visionary leaders. You have led by example! Thank you to the Contend Team. You really are World Changers and History Makers!

A special thanks to my family in Tennessee and Texas, Mom, Laura, David, and Michelle. You inspire me to be more like Jesus! I'm grateful for my mom's side of the family, the Chesshir clan. Thank you, Haskell and Enid Chesshir, who are in the great cloud of witnesses for your service to the Kingdom in serving 38 years as missionaries to South Korea. Thank you, Sherry, Vicky, Phil, Mark, Rand, and Don. I'm grateful for each of you! A special thanks to my Uncle Rand whom I was named after. Your joy-filled faith and love for the King of Kings has profoundly impacted me and made me a better man!

To my incredible in-laws Larry & Carolyn White who moved from Dallas, Texas to Tennessee for three years to help support our family during the onset of this neurodegenerative disease. Thank you for going the extra mile!

As I end these acknowledgments, I would like to express my incredible love and gratitude for my seven children: Michael, Kanaan, Southern, Isaiah, Jezreel, Tirza, and Bethany Hope, who is in the House of God. I am so proud of each of you! Thank you for weathering the last five years of this storm of life that we have encountered together. Thank you for your resilient faith and attitudes and your servants' hearts as you have washed my feet countless times through your service to me and the family. You are World Changers and History Makers!

To my beautiful wife, Samantha, of 30 years. Thank you for never quitting and never stopping in believing for my healing. Thank you for pouring out your life for our family and the Thai people in the concrete jungle of Bangkok, Thailand for 16 years. Thank you for your tenacity and spirit of adventure in moving seven times in 11 years since we returned to the United States from the mission field.

Thank you for standing in the gap for our adopted daughter Jezreel, and going the distance with her, with literally 100's of doctor's visits in the last 15 years. Thank you for your incredible love for the poor, the marginalized, and the orphan. For taking children out of the slums into our home as foster parents in Thailand. For your willingness to adopt Jezreel from

China, with the foreknowledge of her congenital heart issues. Thank you for writing Jezreel's story in your book about adoption, *Walk With Me*.

You are my best friend. My partner in the Kingdom. Thank you for saying yes to me 30 years ago to take "the road less traveled". I love you. *Je t'aime jusque la lune aller et retour. Je t'aimerai toujours.*

Finally, I would like to thank Jesus my older brother who made a way for me to be reconciled to the Father through His sacrifice. Thank you, Jesus, for saving my life and giving me hope that overcomes every adversity. You are my Healer! Holy Spirit thank you for filling me and leading me every step of the way. Your voice is a constant encouragement to me. Last, I would like to thank my Heavenly Father for creating me and giving me life and breath in my lungs. You're the reason why I live. My life's pursuit is to reflect your love! All glory and honor belong to you!

You are the Fairest of 10,000. The Lover of my soul. The Giver of every good gift. The Alpha and the Omega. The Beginning and the End. You are my Creator. You are my God. My Heavenly Father and my Abba. All my life belongs to you!

Steve Allen
Colorado Springs, Colorado
November 10, 2019

CONTENTS

Foreword   xiii

Preface   xiv

AND HE RAN FOR 40 DAYS

3   Day 1 - The Forty Day Journey

7   Day 2 - Manna from Heaven

11   Day 3 - Mount Zion

15   Day 4 - Mount Sinai

19   Day 5 - The Mountain of God

23   Day 6 - Indefatigable

27   Day 7 - The Steps of a Man

31   Day 8 - The Prayer of Seven

35   Day 9 - What the Dead Don't Do

39   Day 10 - 10,000 Fathers

43   Day 11 - Our Battle Is Not Against Flesh and Blood

47   Day 12 - A Light Set on a Hill

51   Day 13 - Persistent Faith Leads to Wisdom

55   Day 14 - Covenant

59   Day 15 - The Way of the Cross

63   Day 16 - A Cord of Three Strands

67   Day 17 - The Language of God

71   Day 18 - Trust and Obey

75   Day 19 - Perseverance

79   Day 20 - Identity

83   Day 21 - The God Who Answers by Fire

87   Day 22 - The Crucible of Delayed Answers

93   Day 23 - As You Go, Preach the Kingdom!

97   Day 24 - His Ways Are Above Our Ways

101 Day 25 - Whisper

105 Day 26 - Elijah Was a Man Just Like Us!

109 Day 27 - The Battle on the Mountain and in the Valley

113 Day 28 - Obedience Is Greater Than Sacrifice

117 Day 29 - Sonship

121 Day 30 - He Knows Your Name

125 Day 31 - The Rock

129 Day 32 - The Seven Thousand

133 Day 33 - Running Out of Yourself

137 Day 34 - What Are You Doing Here, Elijah?

141 Day 35 - A New Set of Glasses

145 Day 36 - Faithfulness

149 Day 37 - An Upside-Down Kingdom

153 Day 38 - They Will Run and Not Grow Weary

157 Day 39 - Burn the Plow

161 Day 40 - Chariots of Fire

APPENDIX

Postscript: A word from Rand Chesshir

Tribute for the Thailand Mission Team

Endorsements

Seven Kingdom Treasures from the Life of Elijah

Word of Encouragement

Allen Family Ministry Books

Steve Allen's Vision Statement

The Christian life is established through progressive maturity, much like it is described in the life of Jesus: He was perfected through His sufferings. Jesus instructs us in Matthew 10:38 that if we want to be considered His disciples, we must be willing to share His cross and experience it as our own. This is a very sobering thought that many do not contemplate.

I have known Steve Allen for the better part of three decades. I have observed him on top of the mountain and down in the valley. As the hardships of life have assaulted him, I have seen him persevere in faith. In the midst of battles, he stands like an oak of righteousness. As storms rage around him, he remains steadfast to the truth that he has written on the tablet of his heart. This has not happened by chance. He has purposed within his heart to make God's truth his foundation. This truth comforts and guides him as he continues to blaze a trail where many never walk.

Come walk this journey with Steve. The Apostle Paul says, "I want you to pattern your lives after me, just as I pattern mine after Christ" (1 Corinthians 11:1 TPT). The writings within this book are sage advice from one who, much like Paul, can offer lessons learned through personal struggles and victories as he has followed the teachings of Christ. You can pattern your life after Steve because he is a mighty man of God.

2 Corinthians 4:7-9 (TPT) says, "We are like common clay jars that carry this glorious treasure within, so that the extraordinary overflow of power will be seen as God's, not ours. Though we experience every kind of pressure, we're not crushed. At times we don't know what to do, but quitting is not an option. We are persecuted by others, but God has not forsaken us. We may be knocked down, but not out." Steve understands this. He displays this in his daily life. He shares the encouraging and invaluable nuggets he has mined with us. Thank you, Steve, for sharing your heart with us. May these words bless each of us as God leads us down our own journey of life.

Peace, Clint McDowell
Businessman, author, minister, husband, and dad

WHEN LIFE DOES NOT TURN OUT AS PLANNED

I lay on the hospital bed in the exam room staring up at the ceiling. It was August 31, 2015 and I was at Vanderbilt Hospital in Nashville, Tennessee. I had gone through a series of tests over a week and now was reaching the finish line. I would find out that day what my diagnosis and prognosis was going to be from the medical experts.

My left leg had slowly been losing strength over the previous year, and I had developed foot drop in my foot. I could no longer hold it up. The muscles had stopped responding. I lay there looking up at the ceiling, and spoke in my heart, "God, this would be a really good time to hear your audible voice."

Silence.

A thousand thoughts raced through my mind. What was going to happen? How would this affect my wife, family, our ministry, and my future? After what seemed like an hour, the two doctors walked back in and said, "We conferred with another senior colleague and are sorry to say that we believe from the testing that you have ALS - Amyotrophic Lateral Sclerosis."

I asked, "What is the prognosis?"

"There is no treatment available at this time," the doctor responded. "Life expectancy is 3-5 years."

This was not what I had expected for my life, my dreams and calling, my destiny. Over the next week I shared the news with my wife, family, and close friends and pressed into the Lord. What was God saying in the midst of this?

I am with you.
I will never forsake you.
I will fortify and strengthen you.
Trust me.

Throughout those early days, I felt His Shalom, His peace. I felt His presence and His kindness. I did not spend much time asking why. I took hold of the Word, the Living Word, meditating, memorizing, and praying it. I spoke out loud the Word throughout the day. It sustained me and gave me great hope. The Written Word led me to the Living Word. The Living Word is Jesus. He is my hope. My anchor. My life and my next breath.

~~~~

Let me take you back to the summer before my diagnosis. In July of 2014, I helped to lead a summer ministry training school with Caleb Company, the ministry I was working with. In preparation to go to Israel, we spent one month in the States studying God's heart for Israel, taking hold of His plan for us in our identity and destiny, and then pressing into Him through daily prayer and worship.

On the second day of our arrival into Israel, the Gaza War broke out and we came face to face with the stark reality that Israelis face every day; they are surrounded by their enemies. During the thirty days we were in the land, we experienced three air raids and a car exploding into flames by the hands of a radical war protestor a few hundred feet from where our team was standing. We also, however, experienced some amazing ministry opportunities such as taking food to single Russian Jewish immigrant mothers and their children in the city of Ashdod, only 26 miles from where rockets were being shot out of Gaza on a daily basis. We met and prayed with Holocaust survivors and shared our faith with two Jewish orthodox women in a Jerusalem park.

Jerusalem is a city of hills and when in the city, you do a great deal of walking. I started to notice that my left foot was growing heavy. It felt like lead as I walked the pathways of the narrow city streets. I did not think much of it until we left Israel. Our airline canceled all of their flights out of Tel Aviv just one day before we were to fly out due to the missile attacks that were getting closer and closer to the airport. One of our staff members spent two hours on the phone scrambling to get our team of over 20 students and staff on different flights back to the States.

I was part of the team that ended up flying through Toronto, Canada. As we arrived late, we sprinted down a concourse trying to make our connecting flight. I was running down one of the moving sidewalks, a heavy backpack on my back, when the toe of my left sandal caught the lip of the end of the sidewalk and I went sprawling. I ended up on my face; dazed and looking down, I found I had bloodied my left knee. Shocked and befuddled, I knew something was amiss; this was not normal.

We finally made it back home to Nashville and I started treatment with a chiropractor and a muscle therapist. Five months later there was no improvement and I began to wonder if there was something more sinister going on. Something I was not expecting...

~~~~

After Elijah had experienced an incredible victory over the enemies of God on top of Mount Carmel, he got down on his knees and hands and in a birthing position prayed through until the breakthrough. He saw through his servant's eyes, appearing on the horizon, a single rain cloud and he knew in his heart that after 3 ½ years of drought, the rains were coming. Elijah then tucked in his robe and ran to the capital of Samaria outrunning King Ahab and his chariot of horses.

The title of this 40-day devotional journal is, *And He Ran for 40 Days*.

It does not state this implicitly in the text of 1 Kings. The scripture uses the word traveled. I chose this title because I am a runner. Elijah was a runner too. He outran King Ahab's chariot to the city of Jezreel. I grew up running with my father in high school. I can remember distinctly running the Peachtree 10K with my dad and 25,000 people the summer of 1979. I ran in college and immensely enjoyed the time talking to the Lord on those quiet runs. When we went to the mission field in Thailand, I joined a Thai jogging team in our neighborhood. Over the next ten years, I took my two oldest sons on a number of 10Ks around the capital city of Bangkok. There's something about running that cultivates time and space to commune with our Heavenly Father. After a few miles, the body starts to relax, and your legs fall into a natural rhythm. The mind opens up to rich contemplative prayer and hearing His voice. One of my life verses is out of the Psalms:

I run in the path of your commands, for you set my heart free!

Psalm 119:32 (NIV)

With the onslaught of ALS, I've not been able to run for the last five years. This title is a declaration of hope and faith for me. A prophetic statement that I will run again.

Steve Allen
Colorado Springs, Colorado

Note: 50% of the profits from this 40-day devotional will be sown into missions and funding adoptions.

"THEREFORE, SINCE WE ARE SURROUNDED BY SUCH A GREAT CLOUD OF WITNESSES, LET US THROW OFF EVERYTHING THAT HINDERS AND THE SIN THAT SO EASILY ENTANGLES. AND LET US RUN WITH PERSEVERANCE THE RACE MARKED OUT FOR US, FIXING OUR EYES ON JESUS, THE PIONEER AND PERFECTER OF FAITH. FOR THE JOY SET BEFORE HIM HE ENDURED THE CROSS, SCORNING ITS SHAME, AND SAT DOWN AT THE RIGHT HAND OF THE THRONE OF GOD."

HEBREWS 12:1-2 NIV

AND HE
RAN
FOR 40 DAYS

STEVE ALLEN

Half Moon Bay in California

"For behold, I create new heavens and a new earth; And the former things will not be remembered or come to mind. But be glad and rejoice forever in what I create; For behold, I create Jerusalem for rejoicing And her people for gladness." Isaiah 65:17-18 NASB

DAY 1

THE FORTY DAY
JOURNEY

Elijah was afraid and ran for his life. When he came to Beersheba in Judah, he left his servant there, while he himself went a day's journey into the wilderness. He came to a broom bush, sat down under it and prayed that he might die. "I have had enough, Lord," he said. "Take my life; I am no better than my ancestors." Then he lay down under the bush and fell asleep. All at once an angel touched him and said, "Get up and eat." He looked around, and there by his head was some bread baked over hot coals, and a jar of water. He ate and drank and then lay down again. The angel of the Lord came back a second time and touched him and said, "Get up and eat, for the journey is too much for you." So he got up and ate and drank. Strengthened by that food, he traveled forty days and forty nights until he reached Horeb, the mountain of God.

1 Kings 19:3-8 NIV

After Elijah defeats the 450 prophets of Baal on Mount Carmel through a spectacular display of the power of God, a death threat from the wicked queen Jezebel sends him into the desert, fleeing for his life.

Depressed, deflated, and filled with self-doubt, an exhausted Elijah falls to the ground and wants to die. An angel of the Lord comes to him, giving him food and water, and watches over him while he rests. After a deep sleep, he rises and then under the strength of the Lord, Elijah travels 40 days and 40 nights to Mount Horeb/Mount Sinai – the Mountain of God – to encounter the Living One.

In the Bible, the number 40 is significant. It represents a time of testing. Moses was 40 days on top of Mount Sinai to receive the Commandments of the Lord for God's people. Israel wanders in the desert for 40 years, disciplined for their grumbling and complaining. Jesus was 40 days fasting in the wilderness in preparation to receive the mantle of His ministry to preach the Kingdom of God to Israel, to become the bridge between darkness and light, death and life. In my battle with ALS, I am five years in this wilderness journey, in a fight for my life. It is the equivalent of forty-five 40-day trials. Some days, I want to throw in the towel and quit. In the midst of these trials, God is ever present. His name is Emanuel, God with us. Almost weekly, I receive courage to have faith for breakthrough and to persevere. To date, I have received 49 dreams in five years from many friends and family who have seen me healed and walking.

REFLECTION:

What testing have you gone through? What have you learned about perseverance, faithfulness, and obedience to the Lord through that testing? James says we are to count it pure joy when we face trials and hardships (James 1:2-3). My friend, do not quit your assignment. Do not give up your post. Do not quit the race you have been called to run. He is the Faithful One! He will see you through!

PRAYER:

Father, teach me to number my days that I might gain a heart of wisdom (Psalm 90:12). Teach me to turn to you in the midst of my trials that I might gain heart-strength and overcome the lies and deception of the enemy. I know that what I fear, I empower. Teach me to fear You above all things! I love you Abba!

JOURNAL:

DAY 2

MANNA FROM HEAVEN

When Elijah saw how things were, he ran for dear life to Beersheba, far in the south of Judah. He left his young servant there and then went on into the desert another day's journey. He came to a lone broom bush and collapsed in its shade, wanting in the worst way to be done with it all — to just die: "Enough of this, God! Take my life—I'm ready to join my ancestors in the grave!" Exhausted, he fell asleep under the lone broom bush.

1 Kings 19:3-5 MSG

The quieter you become, the more you can hear.

Anonymous

On June 1st, 2017 during a morning prayer time, I heard in my spirit, "*And He Ran for 40 Days.*" I knew immediately it was a reference to the story of Elijah and how, after a stunning victory over the demonic prophets of Baal, Elijah ran. He escaped to the desert and asked God to end his life. He was physically and emotionally exhausted after the epic battle over the prophets of Baal. He had pulled from all his resources and reserves and was now empty. He had nothing more to give. He had come to the end of his finite self.

In Hebrews 4:11, God speaks to us through the voice of the Apostle Paul that we are to make every effort to enter into the rest of God. Ironic, is it not? We have to work very hard to rest!

One of my spiritual fathers, Don Finto, shared a valuable teaching to a group of young pastors and leaders almost twenty years ago. In his teaching, he said to guard your heart and be aware of your own flesh when in these situations: while traveling to a new city, after a geographical move, and after a great ministry experience when you are riding on a spiritual high.

The enemy is shrewd. He seeks opportune times to attack us or tempt us. The enemy waited until near the end of the 40 days when Jesus was in the desert fasting. He waited until Jesus was weakest physically. What is the answer to these attacks of the enemy? The Living Word of God, prayer, and seeking to be in the presence of our Father. These are a few of the most powerful weapons of God. What else? We are to strive mightily to enter into His rest. In His rest we are renewed, refreshed, and rejuvenated. When we enter into His rest, we receive the gift of humility. How?

In humility, we acknowledge that we are not God, but He is! Humility keeps the focus on Him and not on ourselves. We are to point others to Him and not to ourselves. Humility keeps us from the cult of the individual, of the idolatry of allowing others to put us on a pedestal. It feels good to have the adulation and praise of men, as it appeals to our flesh. The praise of man is dangerous. When we are on a pedestal, we become enamored with our own self. We are the man of the hour and the go-to person. It is a precarious place and only a matter of time before we fall off that pedestal. As the well-known proverb states, "Pride comes before a fall."

It is under the broom tree in the solitude of the desert that Elijah encounters the presence and the kindness of Jehovah God. He cries out to God, "I am no better than my ancestors!" "Just kill me." "Woe is me!" Here we see the amazing response and nature of our God, His compassion and love.

The angel of the LORD appears to him and feeds him bread and water. Weary to the bone, exhausted, depleted, and famished, Elijah is fed by the Hand of God. I imagine what Elijah might have heard in that place. *Rest, my son.* Elijah falls into a deep sleep. He awakes. *Eat, my son.* Elijah eats of the living bread and the living water that Father God provides for him. It is then that Elijah is able to travel supernaturally for 40 days and 40 nights sustained by the Bread of Heaven.

REFLECTION:

Recall a time when you were bone-weary and exhausted from life's challenges. How did you respond to that trial? What does it look like to enter into the rest of the Lord? How do we learn to rest in such a frenetic and busy culture?

PRAYER:

Abba Father, thank you that you call us into your rest to experience your presence, healing, and love. Thank you, Jesus, that you are the Bread of Life that sustains us!

JOURNAL:

DAY 3

MOUNT ZION

Who may ascend the hill of the Lord? Who may stand in His holy place? He who has clean hands and a pure heart, who does not lift up his soul to an idol or swear by what is false.

Psalm 24:3-4 NIV

Elijah climbed mountains. He battled demonic forces on Mount Carmel and met with the living God on Mount Horeb. It hit me recently that Mount Horeb and Mount Sinai are one and the same. I have climbed many mountains in the past and look forward to the day where I can climb again!

Now, years into my battle with the giant of ALS, my muscles have atrophied, and my legs no longer work. I am grateful for the use of a power wheelchair that allows me to continue to be mobile. My sons and good friends take me to a gym three times weekly to do swim therapy to exercise my legs. I have not run in dozens of months. Stairs are now my equivalent of Mt. Everest.

Logically, it does not seem realistic to think that I will be able to climb a mountain again, but God is not bound to logic! He is the God of the impossible; He is the God of miracles. He is Jehovah Rapha, our Great

Healer. He is also known as the Word. The Word of God is a living seed that, planted in our heart, bears fruit. It bears the fruit of hope and faith in me that I will climb mountains again.

It has been said, "Between the promise and the palace is the process." In the process, I continue to teach, mentor, and disciple young leaders in our ministry. I thoroughly enjoy leadership coaching with my coaching business. I continue to write, and this 40-day devotional journal that you hold in your hand is fruit of that.

In July of 2017, I flew to Israel and stayed at our ministry's apartment in Jerusalem. It sits on a steep hill overlooking the Hinnom Valley and Mount Zion, the "Hill of the Lord". This is probably the same mountain that David wrote about in Psalm 24. I love the roof of the apartment because I can pray over Jerusalem and set my eyes on the Mount of Olives where Jesus will return. Each morning when I decree my vision statement out loud, I include the following: "As a watchman for Israel, I stand on her walls and in the spirit, cry out for her salvation day and night until a mighty river of revival flows through the earth."

We are instructed to pray for the peace of Jerusalem. Why? Israel is the apple of God's Eye. The Jewish people are Jesus' blood family. The majority do not yet know Him. Paul shares in Romans 11:12, "But if their transgression means riches for the world, and their loss means riches for the Gentiles, how much greater riches will their fullness bring!" He is returning. He is coming back to make his home with us. Jews and Gentiles, we will be together.

In January 2019, I received a text from an intercessor who was staying at a ministry apartment that overlooks Mount Zion. She was awakened at 1:11 a.m. and stood on the balcony praying over Jerusalem. She prayed for me and said that she believes that I will climb Mount Zion again!

REFLECTION:

What journey has God asked you to travel? What is your destination at this hour? What is a dream for which you are contending and interceding? Take five minutes to listen to the Lord and journal what you receive from Him.

PRAYER:

Father God, thank you that each and every day my faith is growing and belief is rising in my heart to believe you for the impossible! You are the God of Elijah. You are the God of Israel. And you are the Lord of my life!

JOURNAL:

California Redwood Grove

"Let the heavens be glad, and let the earth rejoice; Let the sea roar, and all it contains; Let the field exult, and all that is in it. Then all the trees of the forest will sing for joy Before the LORD, for He is coming, For He is coming to judge the earth. He will judge the world in righteousness And the peoples in His faithfulness." Psalm 96:11-13 NASB

DAY 4

MOUNT SINAI

The Lord said, "Go out and stand on the mountain in the presence of the Lord, for the Lord is about to pass by."

1 Kings 19:11 NIV

When God called Elijah to Mount Horeb, he called him on a journey to meet face-to-face with the living God. God revealed Himself to Moses there on that mountaintop, in the burning bush, and now hundreds of years later He will appear to Elijah. Mountaintops represent a shift in vision, a new perspective in seeing the landscape around us. He wants us to have His eyes, His vision to see the world.

Soon after I started to write this 40-day devotional on the life of Elijah, the Holy Spirit reminded me of a prophetic word that I received 15 years ago. In 2004, I was on the mission field in Bangkok, Thailand and received a word from a visiting minister who traveled to Thailand every year:

"You will climb Mount Sinai at sunrise and God will confirm His word to you."

At the time, I had no idea the meaning of this word or the relevance to me. Now, looking back, I have deeper understanding and a sense of its weight.

I love mountains! From an early age, I loved climbing mountains and seeing for miles around. From the heights you see incredible vistas and gain new perspectives. I grew up on a mission compound in Seoul, South Korea that was built on the side of a hill. As a child, I remember many times sitting on the hill looking down into the valley, daydreaming of great adventures. Later in Boy Scouts, some of my most memorable camping trips involved mountains, such as an international Jamboree with scouts from four nations, camping together in the mountains north of Seoul. Then, as a teenager, I remember hiking up Stone Mountain in Georgia. Finally, during my senior year in high school, I will never forget a 10-day scouting trek with my father and seven young men on the Appalachian Trail, part of a 2,000 mile stretch that runs on the back of the mighty Appalachian Mountains from Georgia to Maine.

In 1997, I trekked the Annapurna Sanctuary in Nepal with a college buddy of mine, a fulfillment of a lifelong dream. The dream was to trek the Himalayas on what is known as the Roof of the World. During the trek, I dreamed of taking my sons there one day when they were older. This dream was realized in November of 2006 when I led a trek into the Everest region with two of my best friends and our sons. The apex of this adventure was taking communion together at the top of a pass on the trail, looking across a valley at the face of Mt. Everest, the highest peak on earth. As we finished our communion, to our utter astonishment and great delight a white eagle swooped down over our heads into the valley below. We scrambled with our cameras trying to get a picture but missed it! We will never forget that moment, frozen in time, etched in our memories!

REFLECTION:

What experiences have you had on mountaintops? What has the Lord revealed to you about His nature on these high places? What metaphorical mountain are you currently climbing in your life?

PRAYER:

Thank you, Father God that you are sovereign over all the earth and all the affairs of men. Thank you that even though I'm only one in over seven billion people on the planet, you know me by name. You know my thoughts even before I speak them.

JOURNAL:

DAY 5

THE MOUNTAIN OF GOD

He who forms the mountains, who creates the wind, and who reveals his thoughts to mankind, who turns dawn to darkness, and treads on the heights of the earth — the Lord God Almighty is his name.

Amos 4:13 NIV

Fear always makes you run. What happened to make Elijah, who had audacious courage and faith, and saw God's mighty power displayed with fire from heaven on Mount Carmel, melt in trepidation and flee? It is a matter of six inches, the distance our eyes move from looking to God in the heavens to looking horizontally to man in front of us. If we elevate the fear of man over the fear of God, we will abandon our post and run. Faith or fear, whatever we focus on we empower.

In the summer of 2017, I returned from a week in Israel with our Caleb Ministry Training School of 17 students and intern leaders. We traveled from Jerusalem to Kiriyat Shmona in the far north. We did outreach in the kibbutz of the Golan and on the boardwalk in Tiberius on the Sea of Galilee. From there I went with one of our teams far south to Kadesh Barnea on the Egyptian border. We stayed in the home of a fiery believer named Avishai, a Yeminite Jew; his Dutch wife Yolanda; and their five children. Avishai reminds me of Elijah. A man of God full of fire and of the Spirit who is contending with the darkness in the Land, praying for the sick and the lost, and seeing people touched by the Spirit of the Living God.

Avishai prayed for my healing from ALS for several hours the night we first arrived. Passionate and full of faith, Yolanda quietly prayed in the background, adding words of encouragement and stories of faith. In the midst of the prayer session they spoke of Mount Sinai nearby and of a prophet friend of theirs from Africa who had been there in the Spirit. (It is 15 miles away in the Sinai desert of Egypt.) The next evening, they took me in their van to the border fence; from a raised knoll in their compound, with Egypt only a mile away, they showed me the mountain in the distance, a rounded hill. Not very impressive but in line with what the word Sinai means. They shared an article with me by a scholar who believes this mountain is the actual Mountain of God where Moses met God in a burning bush and received the Ten Commandments. It is where Elijah met with Adonai. The proximity of this mountain is more in line with the timetable of the Children of Israel leaving Egypt and traveling eleven days into the wilderness to Kadesh Barnea. Traditional locations of Mount Sinai are much further away in Saudi Arabia in remote and difficult places to reach. It would have taken the Children of Israel, three million in number, many more days to reach those locations. I look forward to climbing Mount Sinai when I am healed!

REFLECTION:

Think back over your life and identify seasons of testing. What did you learn from these seasons? What character was developed in you? Most of us do not like to be tested and tried but it is where the gold is forged in our lives. Take time to journal what gold has been produced in your life through trials.

PRAYER:

Father God, as I walk in the footsteps of your son Jesus, help me to have the resolve and character to embrace hardship and suffering as Jesus did. Give me a heart of gratitude for all that you have done in my life. Thank you that you are working in my heart to conform me to the likeness of your son Jesus (Romans 8:28-29).

JOURNAL:

DAY 6

INDEFATIGABLE

The power of the Lord came on Elijah and, tucking his cloak into his belt, he ran ahead of Ahab all the way to Jezreel.

1 Kings 18:46 NIV

The distance from Mount Carmel to the city of Jezreel is approximately 17-30 miles according to scholars. It is quite significant that Elijah under the power of God was able to outrun King Ahab and his chariot of horses. Only a few days later Elijah, again under the power of God, travels supernaturally 40 days and 40 nights without food or water to the Mountain of God, Mount Horeb.

Webster's dictionary defines indefatigable as incapable of being fatigued. This is a great word, but in reality, eventually everyone tires and must rest. It is in the rest of God that we find our greatest strength. John 15 says that we must abide in the vine. In this narrative of Elijah experiencing a great victory and elation on top of the mountain, he is quickly brought back to the ground as he runs for his life into the desert. It is important to point out that Elijah the prophet and Elijah the man are one and the same. We can take courage from this as we walk through life. Elijah was flesh and blood just as we are. The key is to keep our eyes on the Father!

In my own life, in this battle with ALS, I experienced great hope for breakthrough when I was able to meet a prominent doctor in Jerusalem in April of 2016. He was doing cutting edge research with MS and ALS, and I was told I was a potential candidate for their study. After waiting for three months an Israeli friend of mine made a phone call and found out the door was shut. Where does our hope lie? How do we persevere through the ups and downs of contending for breakthrough with an evil giant like ALS? Through indefatigable perseverance and hope, not based on man or medical facts, but upon the promises of God and His enduring presence. It has been said there are facts and then there is truth.

The truth of God is greater than the facts.

As sons and daughters of the Most-High God we are called to persevere. To go the distance. To take our stand and not shrink back. What must we have in order for us to stay faithful to Jesus? We must have relationship with Him. We must know Him and be known by Him. He knows our name. He knows our thoughts, our fears, and our joys. He is for us and not against us.

Our present trials? Allow them to catapult you closer to Jesus. Hold fast to Him in the storm. He will not let you down! Just this morning I received a call and text from two more people who have had dreams of my healing. This has encouraged me to steward the word of the Lord over my life (1 Timothy 1:18).

Charles Spurgeon said this, "I kiss the waves that slam me against the Rock of Ages." We stand on the rock in the storm. The rock is Jesus. He is our strong tower. He is the Faithful One. He will never let us down!

REFLECTION:

What challenges are you facing in this season? What sobering facts are staring you down on the road of life? How are you standing on His truth? How are you standing on His promises? What does it look like abiding in His rest and in His presence?

PRAYER:

Thank you, Abba that you have invited me into your rest, into a John 15 abiding, in your presence and in your love. Thank you that you have overcome death, disease, and bondage on the cross. Thank you that you have lifted up your standard of the cross against the onslaught of the enemy. Thank you for your indefatigable love for us!

JOURNAL:

DAY 7

THE STEPS OF A MAN

Listen, my son, accept what I say, and the years of your life will be many.
I instruct you in the way of wisdom and lead you along straight paths.
When you walk, your steps will not be hampered;
when you run, you will not stumble.

Proverbs 4:10-12 NIV

How many miles did Elijah travel in those 40 days? How many steps did he make? With every step, I believe Elijah was working through the pain in his heart, the disappointment of not seeing revival break out in Israel. It takes time to work through these emotions. There are times we need to go on a 40-day journey. To seek the face of God. To work out our faith. To remind ourselves what God is doing in our lives and of His unchangeable and immutable nature.

Over the past few years, I have experienced the weakening of my legs with the impact of ALS. My nervous system has been slowly shutting down, no longer sending electrical impulses to the muscles in my legs. The muscles have been atrophying and my steps have ceased. Two years ago, I had two leg braces and walked with a cane. For longer distances I used a rollator, a walker with wheels. Now I am using an electric power chair and can no longer walk. My sons and my wife take turns dressing me in the morning and helping me into bed at night.

Why is this happening to me?

Job asked this question and was answered with the rock solid eternal assurance of God. God is not the author of evil. We live in a fallen world and the impacts of Adam's choice. We ask God our Father for healing and stand on prophetic words for breakthrough. In the interim we live by hope and faith. Two years ago, every step I took was deliberate. I watched carefully the ground in front of me, aware of any dips in the path or any obstacles in the way. Through this journey, I have become more aware of how the scripture speaks of the steps of man.

He will not let your foot slip. Psalm 121:3

Though a righteous man falls seven times, he rises again. Proverbs 24:16

He brought me out into a spacious place. Psalm 18:19

He enables me to stand on the heights. Psalm 18:33

When you walk, your steps will not be hampered; when you run, you will not stumble. Proverbs 4:10-12

These scriptures are paraphrased in the words of the author.

REFLECTION:

The steps of a man are often a metaphor for his walk of faith. God is a good Father. He sustains us, provides for us, listens to us, holds us, and loves us.

He is Elohim, the Name that is above every name. He is Emanuel, God with us. He is with me in this valley. He is with you in yours. Keep walking. Keep trusting Him. Keep the faith. Do not waver in the goodness and the love of the Father. Journal how God has watched over your steps during seasons of your life.

Even though I walk through the valley of the shadow of death, I will fear no evil for you are with me; your rod and your staff, they comfort me. Psalm 23:4

PRAYER:

Father, God, I don't understand why some things happen in life. I humble myself under your loving hand. I thank you for the breath in my lungs. I thank you for giving me life. It is a precious gift from you. I choose to thank you in my valley, the place of waiting and contending and believing. My highest praise comes from my lowest valley. In the name of life itself, Yeshua, the Savior of all mankind. Amen.

JOURNAL:

DAY 8

THE PRAYER OF SEVEN

And Elijah said to Ahab, "Go, eat and drink, for there is the sound of a heavy rain." So Ahab went off to eat and drink, but Elijah climbed to the top of Carmel, bent down to the ground and put his face between his knees. "Go and look toward the sea," he told his servant. And he went up and looked. "There is nothing there," he said.
Seven times Elijah said, "Go back."
The seventh time the servant reported, "A cloud as small as a man's hand is rising from the sea."
So Elijah said, "Go and tell Ahab, 'Hitch up your chariot and go down before the rain stops you'."
Meanwhile, the sky grew black with clouds, the wind rose, a heavy rain started falling and Ahab rode off to Jezreel. The power of the Lord came on Elijah and, tucking his cloak into his belt, he ran ahead of Ahab all the way to Jezreel.

1 Kings 18:41-46 NIV

God is looking for faithfulness amongst his people on the earth. In the spirit, Elijah heard the rain coming. In the natural, he had to press through until the breakthrough. Elijah interceded until heaven invaded earth and the rains fell. Not once, not twice, but seven times Elijah prayed and then sent his servant to look to the horizon to see if the rains were coming. What if Elijah had stopped at the sixth time?

Seven represents completion and perfection in the Word of God. The seven days of creation. The seven Spirits of God. The seven churches in Revelation. The seven lampstands. Elisha tells Naaman the Syrian general to wash seven times in the Jordan for the cleansing of his leprosy. At the end of his life, Elisha tells Jehoash the king of Israel to take in his hand arrows and strike the ground, symbolic of victory over his enemies. The king strikes the ground only three times. He did not go the distance; he did not complete activating his faith as God wanted him to.

In my own life, I am learning the power of persistent prayer. To not give up in asking God for breakthrough in my own life for a healing miracle. In Luke 18, Jesus teaches the disciples to pray with the story of the persistent widow. In this narrative, He shares how the widow came day after day to the unjust judge to plead her case. She was poor. She was a woman. She was a widow. In Middle Eastern culture, in that day, it was three strikes against her. She had no influence. She had no money to sway this earthly court, but she was persistent! Jesus tells his disciples this parable "to show them that they should always pray and not give up" (Luke 18:1).

REFLECTION:

What current life situation are you in now that requires persistent prayer? Have you prayed through to the seven? Don't give up! Be persistent in prayer.

PRAYER:

Father God, thank you that you answer our prayers! Thank you that you give us faith and tenacity to go the distance in intercession. Thank you that you've taught us to pray through to the breakthrough!

JOURNAL:

DAY 9

WHAT THE DEAD DON'T DO

When Elijah saw how things were, he ran for dear life to Beersheba, far in the south of Judah. He left his young servant there and then went on into the desert another day's journey. He came to a lone broom bush and collapsed in its shade, wanting in the worst way to be done with it all — to just die: "Enough of this, God! Take my life — I'm ready to join my ancestors in the grave!" Exhausted, he fell asleep under the lone broom bush.

1 Kings 19:3-5 MSG

After the epic victory on top of Mount Carmel, Elijah's world is turned upside down when he is threatened with death. We encounter Elijah exhausted, depleted of hope, weary with battle; he wants to die. When our focus shifts from our Heavenly Father to ourselves, we lose perspective. We think that we are the answer and that the solution lies within us. We lose hope and sink into despair. We need a heavenly alignment! We need to get the focus off of self and onto Him!

In the spring of 2017, the wife of one of my spiritual sons sent me this email to encourage {to infuse with courage} me in my battle with the giant of ALS. No medical cure and given 3-5 years to live, I am now five years into this journey...my "forty day" journey in the wilderness.

Steve,

A couple of times today while I was worshiping, I felt like Papa Yah was reminding me of this for you, so I wanted to share it. It certainly was very impactful for me. A few years ago, I had gotten to Grace Center [our home church] early and decided to sit in the auditorium and wait for worship to start. Quickly after sitting, God said, "Write down in your journal everything the dead don't do." I thought, ok, and began making a list of the things the dead didn't do: the dead don't eat; the dead don't drink; the dead don't sing; the dead don't speak; the dead don't dance; and on and on. After I had made a list, I waited but God didn't say anything. So, I thanked Him for His perspective, told Him this was insightful, and started trying to make meaning of it by comparing what the living do. Yet God still didn't say anything about the list I had made, so I just thanked Him again. Two nights later I had a dream, and all it was, was someone holding a digital clock that read 115:17 and I knew that it was the Psalms. Psalm 115:17 says, "The dead don't praise, nor do those who go down into the pit."

God Bless!

Nikki Weeks

Powerful. I am grateful for those around me who hear the voice of God and share His heart with me. Remember this truth: "The mind of sinful man is death, but the mind controlled by the Spirit is life and peace" (Romans 8:6 NIV, 1984). Satan would have us believe that death is the answer to the trials in our life. The answer to our trials is worship! To worship the Father in the midst of these trials. For He is worthy!

REFLECTION:

When we turn from God and focus on ourselves, we lose hope. There have been times on this journey that I have wearied of the fight and wanted to throw in the towel. Recount a time that you wanted to give up on your journey in life. How has God worked in you, to bring you back to keeping your eyes on Jesus?

PRAYER:

Father God, give me the strength and the tenacity to go the distance in the race that you marked for me! Every day of my life I will choose to praise you and cultivate a heart of gratitude! Thank you that you've given us the ability to open our mouths and worship you!

JOURNAL:

Mauna Kea on The Big Island of Hawaii

"God's glory is on tour in the skies, God-craft on exhibit across the horizon." Psalm 19:1 MSG

DAY 10

10,000 FATHERS

*Behold, I am going to send you Elijah the prophet before the coming of the
great and terrible day of the Lord. He will restore the hearts of the fathers to
their children and the hearts of the children to their fathers, so that I will not
come and smite the land with a curse.*

Malachi 4:5-6 NASB

The role of the prophet is to hear from God and to speak to man on His
behalf. In the days of Israel, Elijah sought to bring the people of Israel back
to the Father. In my day, my heart yearns to see the Joshua generation turn
to the Heart of the Father.

It has been said that the way we view our Heavenly Father is through the lens
of the relationship with our earthly father. I am so grateful that I was blessed
with a great father. He loved well and was a man of wisdom and honor. He
wore many hats, as a lieutenant colonel in the military, veterinarian, 16-year
missionary to South Korea, and an elder in the church. Dad loved my mom
well and they both sowed into us children by raising us to know Jesus.

Time is a precious commodity that once spent is gone. My father invested this commodity intentionally into my life. He spent time with me. As a young boy, we built school science projects together in the downstairs workshop. Dad read books to us growing up. *Swiss Family Robinson. Where the Red Fern Grows. The Other Side of the Mountain.* He became a scout master in order to spend time with me in Boy Scouts. We trekked for 10 days on the Appalachian Trail in Georgia, experiencing the natural beauty of God's creation.

Paul says these words to the church in Corinth: "Even though you have ten thousand guardians in Christ, you do not have many fathers, for in Christ Jesus I became your father through the gospel" (1 Corinthians 4:15 NIV, 1984). One of my main callings in life is to father, to father my own six sons and daughters and to raise up spiritual sons and daughters. My personal vision statement contains these words: My mission...is to raise up 10,000 sons who become 10,000 God-fearing, God-loving fathers who disciple nations in preparation for the return of the King!

In the garden, God the Father walked with Adam and Eve. There was no book, no law, just pure relationship, a Father with his children. When sin entered onto the stage of humanity, the relationship was severed and torn apart. At the core of the Father Heart of God is this one focus, one anthem, one burning quest – to restore us back into relationship with Him!

REFLECTION:

Describe your relationship with your father. What does it look like to walk in a life-giving relationship with Abba and with your earthly father? How do you cultivate relationships with your spiritual and natural families? In what ways would you like to improve those relationships?

PRAYER:

Thank you for revealing your Father Heart to us! Fill us to the tipping point with your presence so that it spills out on the people around us. Help us to reflect your Father Heart to the lost, the poor, and the orphan.

JOURNAL:

OUR BATTLE IS NOT AGAINST FLESH AND BLOOD

*Now Ahab told Jezebel everything Elijah had done and how he had killed
all the prophets with the sword. So Jezebel sent a messenger to Elijah to say,
"May the gods deal with me, be it ever so severely, if by this time tomorrow I
do not make your life like that of one of them."*

1 Kings 19:1-2 NIV

After a mighty display of the power of God on top of Mount Carmel when
the prophets of Baal are killed, Jezebel, the wicked queen of Israel, issues a
death warrant for Elijah. After hearing the news, Elijah runs for his life into
the desert. Elijah had stood as a lone voice, a spokesman for God confronting

the idolatry and iniquity of Israel. In the desert, Elijah is refreshed, renewed, and restored to focusing on God and not the enemy.

In my own battle with ALS, I have received several dreams and prophetic words from intercessors that the root of my sickness is a spiritual curse that was spoken against me from our time in Thailand as missionaries for 16 years.

I have prayed through this and thought of several individuals that might have spoken out against me. The Spirit has reminded me of Ephesians 6:10-20, that our battle is not against flesh and blood but against the powers of this dark world and the spiritual forces of evil in the heavenly realms.

Where does our battle lie?

The scheme of the enemy is to turn us against flesh and blood. Satan hides in the shadow behind deception and lies. We need to identify our true enemy. It is not our fellow brother or sister.

Jesus taught the disciples how to pray in the Beatitudes. In the middle of this prayer he instructs us to forgive our debtors. He goes on to say that if we do not forgive, we will not be forgiven. We must let go of our "right" to judge others and surrender them to the Lord.

REFLECTION:

Have I learned to forgive? Whom do I need to forgive? This is one of the most important and critical tests that we will face in our lifetime; can we forgive those who sin against us? Yes. We forgive because Jesus first forgave us. He set the example for us to follow. In the same way, He gives us the power and the heart to forgive those who have wronged us.

PRAYER:

Abba, forgive me when my love grows cold, my heart grows hard, and I resist your Spirit. Wash away all defilement and lies of the enemy. Give me your heart to forgive those who have wronged me.

JOURNAL:

DAY 12

A LIGHT SET ON A HILL

Arise, shine, for your light has come and the glory of the Lord rises upon you. See, darkness covers the earth and thick darkness is over the peoples, but the Lord rises upon you and his glory appears over you. Nations will come to your light, and kings to the brightness of your dawn.

Isaiah 60:1-3 NIV

There is great brokenness in our land. The enemy has focused his attack on marriage and family. There is a carnage that has spread across the landscape of our society. Sexual immorality. Adultery. Domestic violence. Divorce. Abortion. Covenant in marriage has become a rare word. We must intercede for Father God to restore the hearts of men and women to Himself. When their hearts are restored, they will be able to restore the hearts of their children.

Elijah in the time of Israel was a solitary voice calling Israel back to Yahweh. A prophet standing for the Ways of God. In the time of Jesus, John the Baptist was referred to as an Elijah calling Israel to repentance, to return to

God. Father God is looking for a people who will stand in the gap and like Elijah, shine like a beacon of light set on a hill.

In 2005, my wife Samantha and I adopted a special needs little girl from northern China who was born without a left ventricle in her heart. We had been blessed by the Lord with four healthy children and wanted to bring a child into our home that needed lots of love! We also wanted to be a lighthouse for other people to follow in the incredible Kingdom ministry of adoption. We named her Jezreel which means "Planted by God." God planted her in our family. All of us have been adopted and planted into the family of God! We, in turn, have the opportunity to adopt those who have no family. (Read about our adventure of adoption with Jezreel in the book *Walk With Me*, written by my wife, Samantha Allen.)

In Matthew 5:12-14 we're called to be a lamp that shines brightly, a city set on the hill as a beacon of light to all those around. We can help turn our nation back to God through intercession, through fasting, proclamation, serving, and adoption. We are to let our lights shine before the world!

REFLECTION:

Father God, what can I do this day to stand in the gap? What is my role in our day? How can I help turn our nation back to God?

PRAYER:

Father, give me courage to be a voice in my generation. A voice calling out your love to a rebellious and broken world. Give me courage to be a light shining on a hill.

JOURNAL:

PERSISTENT FAITH LEADS TO WISDOM

So do not throw away your confidence; it will be richly rewarded.
You need to persevere so that when you have done the will of God, you will
receive what he has promised. For, "In just a little while, he who is coming
will come and will not delay." And, "But my righteous one will live by faith.
And I take no pleasure in the one who shrinks back."
But we do not belong to those who shrink back and are destroyed,
but to those who have faith and are saved.

Hebrews 10:35-39 NIV

Elijah spent three years hidden in a desert valley fed by ravens and drinking from a brook. What did Elijah do for three years? I believe he communed with God and drank deeply from His presence. I believe he interceded on behalf of Israel to turn back to God. When we spend time in God's presence, we receive His heart. We take on His nature and His character. We become what we behold!

In His presence is the fullness of joy.

In His presence is the fullness of faith.

In His presence is the fullness of wisdom.

I have sought to gain wisdom from the Father by immersing myself in His Living Word and spending time in His presence. I am a leadership coach, and often in my coaching sessions with my clients we will stop and have a time of listening prayer to hear from the Heart of the Father. It is powerful what we receive from Him in those times.

Blessed are those who listen to me, watching daily at my doors, waiting at my doorway. For those who find me find life and receive favor from the Lord. Proverbs 8:34-35

REFLECTION:

Where does wisdom come from? How do you grow in wisdom? What is the Lord revealing to you about stewarding wisdom?

PRAYER:

Father, thank you for the amazing opportunity to come before you and hear your voice. Instill in me a radical faith to obey you. Thank you that you revealed to us that the fear of the Lord is the beginning of wisdom. Help us to fear you over all things!

JOURNAL:

DAY 14

COVENANT

Can a woman forget her nursing child, And not have compassion on the son of her womb? Surely they may forget, Yet I will not forget you. See, I have inscribed you on the palms of My hands; Your walls are continually before Me.

Isaiah 49:15-16 NKJV

God showed himself faithful to Elijah. He proved himself as a covenant-keeping God to Elijah by providing for his daily bread in the Kerith Ravine and by answering by fire when Elijah prayed on Mount Carmel.

What is so important about covenant?

The Father made covenant with us through His son. At the last supper Jesus took the cup and said, "Drink from it, all of you. This is my blood of the covenant, which is poured out for many for the forgiveness of sins. I tell you, I will not drink from this fruit of the vine from now on until that day when I drink it new with you in my Father's kingdom" (Matthew 26:27-29 NIV, 1984).

When Jesus shared His cup with His disciples, He made covenant with them through His life and blood. The next day He gave His life for His disciples and for all of mankind.

In the days of King David, close friends would cut covenant by cutting a small incision in their palms, mixing the blood with their friend and then rubbing dirt into the open wound. The wound would heal with a permanent scar that was evident for all to see. When they came face to face with their enemies, they would hold up their hand to show the scar and make known they were in covenant with their brother. The enemy would immediately know that he if did harm to this man, his covenant brother would come after him.[1]

Jesus has us inscribed on the palms of His hands. He has cut covenant with us and still to this day has the scars to prove it.

As a follower of Jesus, I look forward to the Wedding Feast that is coming on the great and glorious day of His return. It is the Wedding Feast of the Bridegroom King and us, His Bride. It will be an exuberant outpouring of great praise and joy. The enemies of God will be destroyed and the great accuser of the brethren will be cast down. No more death. No more tears. The One who keeps covenant with us will come!

REFLECTION:

What does covenant mean? How has God kept his covenant with you? What does it mean for you to walk in covenant with God?

---

[1] Teaching on the sign of the covenant.
Jerry Dirmann, Pastor of The Rock Anaheim.
Los Angeles, California.

DAY 15

THE WAY OF THE CROSS

Then he said to them all: "Whoever wants to be my disciple must deny themselves and take up their cross daily and follow me."

Luke 9:23 NIV

In my lifetime, I've only heard a handful of sermons on the subject of the way of the cross. We are appreciative and grateful for the atonement of Jesus and His sacrifice. But in our modern-day Christian culture we shrink back from embracing the cross of Christ. We cheapen grace when we overlook the great cost our Lord spent to give us salvation.

We must take up our cross daily and follow Him. What does this mean? For Elijah, it meant confronting the apostasy, the idolatry of a wayward people who left their first love in exchange for the idols of the land. Elijah stood as one man against the 450 prophets of Baal.

What is the cross that we are to take up?

Radical obedience to Jesus Christ in the midst of a culture that is vilifying truth and biblical absolutes. We live in an age where evil is being called good and good evil. Where the murder of the unborn and the innocent is trumpeted as a woman's right. Where morality is a negotiable and gender is an individual choice. We must resolve to take a stand. To stand for truth and life. We must speak the truth in love or we will no longer have a voice.

REFLECTION:

What does it look like to take up your cross and follow Jesus this week? What does it mean to take a stand for truth?

PRAYER:

Abba, thank you that you're worthy of denying myself and taking up my cross daily to be your disciple, to be your son or daughter. You're worthy of my life laid down. Thank you, Jesus, for being the ultimate example of One who has taken up the cross. Greater love has no one than this, to lay down his life for his friends! I love you Abba.

JOURNAL:

San Gabriel Mountains in California

"I will lift up my eyes to the mountains; From where shall my help come?
My help comes from the LORD, Who made heaven and earth."
Psalm 121:1-2 NASB

DAY 16

A CORD OF THREE STRANDS

Those who are led by the Spirit of God are sons of God!

Romans 8:14 NIV

The story of the Bible is the story of family. This ancient narrative is set in the context of an epic Middle Eastern love story. The story of Creator God redeeming, reconciling, and calling back His wayward sons to Himself.

When we find Elijah at the beginning of the story, he is hidden away in a valley in the desert, fed by ravens and supplied with water from a brook. Three years Elijah is in solitude. Then the word of the Lord comes to him and he is called to go to a Gentile widow in the town of Zarephath; she is to feed him. After this, God calls Elijah to confront the diabolic idolatry that was reigning over Israel. This leads to the power encounter on Mount Carmel where the solitary prophet Elijah confronts the prophets of Baal and defeats them, ending with their slaughter in the valley. Do you see a common thread through this narrative? Elijah as the prophet of God is often alone. He is not in community with those who fear Yahweh.

Then the tide shifts, as Elijah, at the news of the wicked queen Jezebel's death warrant on his head, runs for his life. How did Elijah lose heart so quickly? Elijah was alone. He saw the world around him through the lens that he was the only one left in Israel who was faithful to God. Isolation bred introspection and self-absorption. Elijah had become egocentric without the fellowship of brothers and the family of Jehovah God.

When Elijah had finished running away from his assignment, he met with God on Mount Horeb, the Mountain of Meeting where Moses had met with God hundreds of years before. Elijah was on holy ground. God asks him, "Why are you here, Elijah?" (1 Kings 19:9b). Elijah's response shows the focus of his heart. "I have been faithful and I am the only one left" (1 Kings 19:10).

When we are the focus, we lose focus on God and the truth. The truth was that there were 7,000 faithful sons and daughters of Abraham that had not bowed the knee to the Baals. This was news to Elijah! God then directs Elijah to go appoint three men who will be empowered, anointed, and commanded by God to confront and destroy the wickedness in the land. Elijah is commanded to anoint Hazel king of Aram, Jehu king over Israel, and Elisha to take up the mantle of Elijah and succeed him as prophet. A cord of three strands is not easily broken! In unity there is strength and power! God raised up a tribe of brothers to confront the idolatry in the land. It is often in the context of family that God weaves his plan. Elijah now had a spiritual son in Elisha to pass on the call of God.

In my own life, there have been times that I've been self-absorbed and self-focused and miserable! Selfishness does not lead to the righteousness of God! I have learned to walk with a Band of Brothers, encouraging and praying for each other. Standing back to back in battles that rage around us. We have been called to walk in family and in community. It is in this place that God does His best work!

REFLECTION:

Are you walking in community? Do you have brothers and sisters that you are walking with as you follow God? God made us for family. Fathers are to raise up sons. Sons are to hold up the arms of their fathers. Journal about the relationships that you have currently. How is God leading you to grow in community?

PRAYER:

Father God, thank you for placing me into a family. My own immediate blood family and the family of God. Thank you for making me wealthy with friends!

JOURNAL:

DAY 17

THE LANGUAGE OF GOD

The Sovereign Lord has given me a well-instructed tongue, to know the word that sustains the weary. He wakens me morning by morning, wakens my ear to listen like one being instructed.

Isaiah 50:4 NIV

The willingness to obey every word from God is critical to hearing God speak.

Henry T. Blackaby

Elijah knew the voice of God. While in the hidden valley in the desert for three years sustained with meat by the ravens and water from the brook, Elijah waited on God. When the Word of the Lord came to him to leave and go to the widow of Zarephath, he was ready. He obeyed and went.

Jesus also knew the voice of His Father. Very early in the morning, while it was still dark, Jesus got up, left the house and went off to a solitary place, where he prayed (Mark 1:35). Prayer is not a monologue, but a dialogue with the living God. He speaks to us in the language of the Spirit. It has been said that Father God does not speak English but Spirit.

He also speaks through nature as represented in Romans 1:20: "For since the creation of the world God's invisible qualities – His eternal power and divine nature – have been clearly seen, being understood from what has been made, so that people are without excuse."

We see and hear Him through His creation. I often feel His presence when I am in nature. In the past, one of my favorite places to be was on top of the Caleb Hill where I worked during the week. The offices for Caleb Company are on a rural, residential setting set on beautiful rolling Tennessee hills. Prophets and intercessors have prayed there for many years and have seen angels standing in watch over this place of meeting with God.

He speaks in dreams. There are many accounts in Scripture in which God speaks to man through dreams and visions. Directional and warning dreams have proven to be very instrumental to the men and women of God. Joseph is instructed to flee the land of Israel with Mary and baby Jesus through a dream in Matthew 2:13. In fact, God gives specific direction to both Joseph and Mary multiple times that preserves their lives and the life of Jesus the son of God. I have received many dreams in the past five years from friends and family of my healing. These dreams are a tremendous source of hope and faith!

How does He speak?

He speaks through His Living Word.
He speaks through pictures and colors.
He speaks through music and sound.
He speaks through fellow Believers.
He speaks through His audible voice.

He speaks through His still small voice in our hearts.
He speaks through His manifested presence in worship.

REFLECTION:

How does the Lord speak to you? Where do you hear Him the best? In what ways has the Lord given you direction and purpose by listening to Him?

PRAYER:

Father God, I posture my heart to listen to your voice and hear from you. Thank you that you are a God that is known by your name, Emanuel, God with us! You're not far off but are very near. Thank you for speaking into my life!

JOURNAL:

DAY 18

TRUST AND OBEY

This is the love of God, to keep His commands. And His commands are not burdensome, for everyone born of God overcomes the world. This is the victory that has overcome the world, even our faith.

1 John 5:3-4 NIV

What is one of God's main love languages? Obedience. Obedience looks like something. When we ask our children to do something, like daily chores, we are training them in righteousness. Sometimes we have to discipline our children because they decide not to do what we ask, or they have a poor attitude. How do we as children of God walk in obedience to the Father with joy and gratitude? We train ourselves in righteousness. Like a child learning to walk over time, we stumble at first, find our feet, and then move forward in confidence.

Elijah was a prophet of God who did amazing exploits in Israel. He walked in obedience to God. He trusted God for the answer. We tend to look at

Elijah as someone super-human. But let's look again. Nestled at the end of the book of James in the fifth chapter stands this single line: "Elijah was a man just like us" (James 5:17a NIV, 1984).

When Elijah ran for his life from the threat of a wicked queen, he did what we sometimes do – he shifted his focus from the Author of Life to the Prince of Death. His vision was so magnified with his adversary that he no longer saw the God of Israel's armies standing above the fray. So he ran. He ran for 40 days. A time of testing and of questioning. Is God still God? Is He really trustworthy?

At the end of the 40 days, standing on Mount Horeb, Elijah once again finds his stride. He finds out that he is not alone. In fact, 7,000 of his fellow Israelites have stood strong in obeying Jehovah God. He receives his assignment from the Lord and turns around. He takes a step of trust and obeys. He returns to the battle.

In my battle with ALS the last five years, there have been times that my faith has ebbed, and my spirit grown weak and weary with waiting. I'm reminded as a son of God to keep my eyes focused on Father God and not my circumstances. Whatever I focus on I will magnify. I choose to magnify my Father! He is the Faithful One in all the earth!

REFLECTION:

Look back on your life and reflect on the times you have run from your call and assignment and the times you have trusted the Lord and obeyed. You may ask, what is the source of trusting the Father? Intimacy with Him and knowing that Father God loves you as His child. Relationship is built at the speed of trust. When you learn His ways you learn to trust His voice.

PRAYER:

Abba, thank you for the gift of my life. The opportunity to walk in relationship with you. I have seen your deeds. I am learning your ways. Fill me with an unwavering faith in you that enables me to trust and obey. You are worthy, Lord!

JOURNAL:

DAY 19

PERSEVERANCE

After six days Jesus took with him Peter, James, and John the brother of James, and led them up a high mountain by themselves. There He was transfigured before them. His face shone like the sun, and His clothes became as white as the light. Just then there appeared before them Moses and Elijah, talking with Jesus.

Matthew 17:1-3 NIV

Three men, Moses, Elijah, and Jesus all had been tested forty days without food. Moses went to the top of Mount Sinai to meet with God and receive the Ten Commandments. He did not eat or drink and was sustained by the Hand of God for almost six weeks. Elijah was in the Negev south of Be'er Sheva for 40 days traveling without food to Mount Horeb. God put His super on Elijah's natural and the supernatural was released. Jesus, after His baptism, was led by the Holy Spirit into the desert for 40 days of testing and preparation to begin His ministry.

In the economy of God, He allows us to be tried by fire to bring out the gold in us. Precious metals such as silver must be heated up multiple times before they are ready for use. Beloved, have you gone through trials in your life?

Have you been in the desert of testing? Have you endured the storms of life? Remember that God is not angry with you; He is for you.

In August of 2015, when I received the diagnosis of ALS and was given 3-5 years to live, I was told no cure, no hope. But God. I have been sustained by His presence, goodness, and love. He is sovereign. He is present. He is in my wife, my children, and my friends. My body is weak but my spirit is strong. I am standing on His promises and His Living Word. I'm choosing to persevere. Do not give up or give in. Winston Churchill's most famous quote of World War II to his people in England was this, "Never, never, never, never give up!"

REFLECTION:

In this world you will have tribulations but be of good cheer, I have overcome the world. John 16:33 NKJV

Consider it pure joy, my brothers, whenever you face trials of many kinds, because you know the testing of your faith develops perseverance. Perseverance must finish its work so that you may be mature and complete, not lacking anything. James 1:2-3 NIV, 1984

Moses counsels us in Psalm 90:12, "Teach us to number our days, so that we may gain a heart of wisdom" (NIV). Journal the trials you have walked through and the growth and character you have gained through these experiences.

PRAYER:

Thank you Father, for trials and testing that strengthen our resolve to gaze upon you, our life source! We know that in the refining fire of these trials, our impurities are burned out and the pure reflection of our Savior begins to shine through!

JOURNAL:

IDENTITY

*Listen to me, you who pursue righteousness and who seek the Lord:
Look to the rock from which you were cut and to the quarry from which you
were hewn.*

Isaiah 51:1 NIV

As a Man of God, Elijah the prophet had to know who he was in his identity. To be the Voice of God to the people and to represent the righteousness of the Almighty, he had to have the moral gravitas to stand for holiness and truth. He ended up standing as one man on Mount Carmel against demon-possessed pagan priests and the rebellious people of Israel. What enabled him to do this? He did not stand alone. He stood upon the Rock, the Rock of Ages.

Our destiny and assignment come from our identity. Our identity does not come from looking at ourselves by being introspective. We find our identity by looking at the One who made us. For we are made in His image. We are to be image-bearers of the Living God. God has planted greatness in us all. He has put the very DNA of Jesus into us. The God Seed.

We are His representatives to not only those living in our generation on the earth in this age but to the spiritual forces of evil in the heavenly realms. We are called to preach the gospel, the Good News of Jesus Christ, to a dying world as we go along the daily path of life (Mark 16:15).

Matthew 10:7-8 also reminds us, "As you go, proclaim this message: 'The kingdom of heaven has come near.' Heal the sick, raise the dead, cleanse those who have leprosy, drive out demons. Freely you have received; freely give."

We as Believers are walking testaments of the love and goodness of God. For some, we might be the only testament they read. Francis of Assisi said this, "Preach the gospel and if necessary, use words."

We are called to do both! To be light and salt, to be a voice to the lost who are sinking in the pit of despair. We truly have the Good News of Jesus Christ that man can be saved, healed, and delivered from the path of destruction.

REFLECTION:

Do you know who you are? Do you know your identity? Do you know that you are a son and daughter of the Living God? When you know who you are, you can walk confidently and boldly in your God-given life assignment to represent Him to the earth. We are the ambassadors of Christ (2 Corinthians 5:20 NIV)!

PRAYER:

Father God, thank you for creating me and giving me life. Thank you for placing eternity in my heart. You said through your son King David, you stooped down to make me great (Psalm 18:35 TPT)! Thank you for making me great so that I might reflect your glory!

JOURNAL:

THE GOD WHO ANSWERS BY FIRE

*So Ahab sent word throughout all Israel and assembled the prophets on
Mount Carmel. Elijah went before the people and said, "
How long will you waver between two opinions? If the Lord is God, follow
him; but if Baal is God, follow him." But the people said nothing.
Then Elijah said to them, "I am the only one of the Lord's prophets left,
but Baal has four hundred and fifty prophets.
Get two bulls for us. Let Baal's prophets choose one for themselves and let
them cut it into pieces and put it on the wood but not set fire to it.
I will prepare the other bull and put it on the wood but not set fire to it.
Then you call on the name of your god, and I will call on the name of the
Lord. The god who answers by fire — he is God."
Then all the people said, "What you say is good."*

1 Kings 18:20-24 NIV

How did Elijah know that God would answer with fire? Had he done this before? I believe Elijah knew the power of God and knew God would show His power before the people of Israel. In the physical, Elijah was outnumbered 450 to 1, but in the spiritual he was backed up by Creator God and the Host of Heaven. In a mighty display of the majesty and the omnipotence of God, fire falls from Heaven and burns up not only the sacrifice, but the wood, stones, and the water that filled the trench around the altar.

The response of the people of Israel is dramatic. They fall on their faces crying, "The Lord – he is God! The Lord – he is God" (1 Kings 18:39).

In my own personal life, this journey in the Valley of the Shadow of Death with ALS has taught me to surrender my life on the altar. To live not for myself but for the King. God is not the author of disease and death. He did not give me ALS but He is allowing my faith to be purified in the crucible of fire through trials and testing. He's burning away my impurities, dross, and self-focus in my life. The words of Paul come to life when I meditate on his passionate plea to the church in Rome: "Therefore, I urge you, brothers, in view of God's mercy to offer your bodies as living sacrifices, holy and pleasing to God, this is your spiritual act of worship. Do not conform any longer to the pattern of this world but be transformed by the renewing of your mind. Then you'll be able to test and approve what God's will is – His good, pleasing and perfect will!" (Romans 12:1-2).

REFLECTION:

What have you put on the altar before the Lord? What are you contending for in persevering prayer to see breakthrough? Father God is faithful! He will see you through.

PRAYER:

Abba, thank you for your miraculous resurrection power! Thank you that you are a God that answers with fire. Thank you for the fire that burns up my impurities so that I can shine for you and reflect your glory! Remind me that no one can see you without being holy! Thank you that the blood atonement of your son Jesus has engulfed me in the pure white robes of His righteousness.

JOURNAL:

Cadillac Mountain on Mount Desert Island in Maine

"In whose hand are the depths of the earth, The peaks of the mountains are His also. The sea is His, for it was He who made it, And His hands formed the dry land. Come, let us worship and bow down, Let us kneel before the LORD our Maker." Psalm 95:4-6 NASB

DAY 22

THE CRUCIBLE OF DELAYED ANSWERS

And the word of the Lord came to him: "What are you doing here, Elijah?"
He replied, "I have been very zealous for the Lord God Almighty.
The Israelites have rejected your covenant, torn down your altars, and put
your prophets to death with the sword.
I am the only one left, and now they are trying to kill me too."
The Lord said, "Go out and stand on the mountain in the presence of the
Lord, for the Lord is about to pass by."

1 Kings 19:9b-11 NIV

Remember the backdrop to this epic story. Elijah had been hiding for three years, alone, praying for Israel in a hidden valley. In the showdown that occurs on top of Mount Carmel, God displays His power and His might to all of Israel, and 450 pagan prophets of Baal take their last breath, slaughtered in the valley below. At this point what do you think was in the heart of Elijah;

what were his thoughts? Now we will see revival come to Israel! All of Israel will return to the Lord!

But did this happen? No! In fact, Elijah runs for his life when Jezebel sends a messenger with a death warrant on his head. At this point, Elijah wants to die. He is bone-weary and exhausted from the spiritual and physical battle that raged around him. What was God teaching Elijah through this trial and ordeal? What did God want Elijah to focus on? God's heart desire was for Elijah to keep his focus on Him and not the circumstances.

Like Elijah, when we cry out for breakthrough, and weeks turn into months, and months turn into years, how do we sustain our faith to go the distance? Life can be unusually cruel and sometimes we get the wind knocked out of us. We stagger through our days trying to make sense of our trials and circumstances. When I was diagnosed with ALS, I was stunned but kept my eyes on Jesus.

Opportunities arose for me to seek help in cutting edge clinics and hospitals around the world in Jerusalem, Israel, and Pocatello, Idaho. After pursuing these opportunities, with no measurable results, I tried many different healing modalities: chelation therapy, hyperbaric oxygen therapy detoxing, inner healing, prayer, and swim therapy. All this was in addition to a plethora of different supplements that focus on cellular health.

In this journey of the past five years, there has not been a time where the weakening has been reversed. I cannot walk and I am reliant upon a powered wheelchair for my daily mobility. My muscles have atrophied to the point I've lost the ability to lift my arms.

In spite of my physical state, I choose to keep my eyes on Jesus; I choose to believe He's my Healer. This choice is not in a vacuum or a void. The Living Word of God is filled with the truth of God as our Healer. As I mentioned earlier, I've received over 49 dreams and visions in the last five years from friends and family who have seen my healing.

I hold onto these dreams.

Lou Engle says, "Dreams are the chapter titles of our future, of the book that He is writing of our lives."

What sustained Joseph in prison for seven years before he got the call to report to Pharaoh in the palace? He kept his faith alive by remembering the dream given to him at the age of 17. He stewarded the prophetic unction of God, the vision of his future. With much of the prophetic, there was no date attached to the Word. He had to remain faithful, day in and day out until the breakthrough came. Who can understand the ways of God? We often want our "why" questions answered. Very seldom does He answer them.

He is much more interested in our character development and who we are becoming rather than our so-called success. As sons and daughters, He wants us to reflect the nature of His son Jesus. He wants us to be the aroma of Yeshua. Just as grapes are crushed to release the wine, so we too are crushed to release the priceless aroma of His presence. He allows us to experience and endure the crucible of the trials of this life so that the flesh can be crucified and the Spirit shine brightly through our broken bodies.

REFLECTION:

Have you experienced the crucible of delayed answers? How have you navigated these trials? How have you sustained and grown in your faith? In the midst of your waiting keep your eyes on Him! He will never fail you. He is the Faithful One! Remember you become what you behold!

PRAYER:

Father God, thank you that in the midst of our trials you are present, and you are faithful. Help us to never give up and never give in. Fill us with a living hope and a living faith that can never be extinguished. Amen!

JOURNAL:

DAY 23

AS YOU GO, PREACH THE KINGDOM!

After a long time, in the third year, the word of the Lord came to Elijah:
"Go and present yourself to Ahab, and I will send rain on the land."
So Elijah went to present himself to Ahab.

1 Kings 18:1-2 NIV

As you go, preach this message, "the Kingdom of God is near."
Heal the sick, raise the dead, cleanse the leper, cast out demons.
Freely you received, freely give.

Matthew 10:7-8

"As you go" is a picture of the man and woman of God in simple obedience to our Father God, living out the Kingdom. Elijah was a man of God who lived this lifestyle. He walked in simple and radical obedience to the will of the Father and the voice of God.

I love the lyrics to a Brian Johnson Bethel worship song: "Where you go, I will go and what you say I will say." This is the picture of Jesus only doing what He saw His Father doing. What if every Believer lived out of this paradigm and walked in this reality? We would transform our culture and communities within our lifetime.

I am inspired by the lives of those who go: missionaries from the early 1800-1900s like William Carey, Hudson Taylor, Adoniram Judson, and Amy Carmichael; modern-day missionaries like Tracy Evans, who ministered to Muslim insurgents in the archipelago of the Southern Philippines; women like Danya Curry and Heather Mercer, missionaries taken captive by the Taliban in Afghanistan in 2001. (Danya and Heather's riveting testimony is told in the book, *Prisoners of Hope.*)

Abraham is also one of my heroes because he listened to the voice of God and left his home to go to the land God had prepared for him. He did not do it perfectly, but he went! He is known as the Father of our Faith because he was willing to go, to sacrifice, and to believe God at His Word.

In my own life, I have sought to make sharing my faith a daily rhythm. Whether it is at the gym telling others the good news about Jesus or on the phone with customer service telling them that Jesus loves them, I want to be light and salt to those who are searching, hungry, and open to the Lord.

REFLECTION:

Wise men still travel. There are times and seasons when God invites us into His-story; He is writing history at this moment. When we step into the story line of God, we step into the realm of miracles and the place of transformation. The epic call of Father God to us echoes out of the halls of history from the prophet Isaiah: Whom shall I send? And who will go for us? (Isaiah 6:8). Is He calling you? Journal today how you can be sharing Jesus with those around you.

PRAYER:

Father God, give me the faith to step out in boldness. Give me the heart and spirit of Abraham to have a childlike faith to answer you when you call me to step out and go.

JOURNAL:

HIS WAYS ARE ABOVE OUR WAYS

*Go at once to Zarephath in the region of Sidon and stay there.
I have directed a widow there to supply you with food.*

1 Kings 17:9 NIV

The ways of God are above our ways. Through the request of Elijah, God held back the rain of heaven for three years, creating a massive drought in Israel. The brook from which Elijah had been drinking dries up and God commands Elijah to go to Zarephath, in Sidon, the land of the Gentiles, a pagan people. Remember that Jezebel the wicked queen was from Sidon. God sends Elijah into the enemy's stronghold to show Elijah and us that He can use anything, even the enemy, to meet our needs.

Think about the context and cultural construct of Israel in which Elijah lived. A widow had no rights and no husband to take care of or support her.

It says in the narrative of 1 Kings 17 that this widow was gathering sticks to cook her last meal. She was destitute. Impoverished. She had nothing left. The ways of God! God sends Elijah to a Gentile woman, a widow that is dirt poor and has no provision. Through this, God is teaching Elijah trust. Remember this axiom of truth: God can do a lot with a little. He can do even more with less and He can do everything with nothing.

The life of Elijah as it relates to the widow and how God provided miraculously for them has intersected my life as I relay the following story to you:

In September of 2017, an opportunity was presented for me to go to Pocatello, Idaho to receive treatment for ALS from a family-run, holistic, alternative medical facility that has been serving patients for 100 years by three generations of the West family. This facility does not take health insurance and we could not afford the $10,000 a month for treatments. However, in similar fashion to Elijah, we believed God was calling me to go. I went and received treatments for four months. A friend from church when I was in high school wrote a check for the first month. I had the opportunity to do staff training for the clinic and afterwards, the owner and director, Dr. Jason West, proposed an exchange of services for the next three months. God provided miraculously for it all!

REFLECTION:

How have you seen this axiom of truth worked out in your life: "His ways are above our ways" (Isaiah 55:8-9)? What have you learned about the nature of God from learning His ways (Psalm 103:7)? How has God called you to trust Him? How has your faith grown as you have trusted him? God is trustworthy!

PRAYER:

Thank you Father God that you teach us dependency on you through trust and obedience. Thank you for sharing with us the story of Elijah and the widow of Zarephath for us to glean and learn from. You are an awesome and amazing God!

JOURNAL:

DAY 25

WHISPER

*The Lord, the Lord, the compassionate and gracious God, slow to anger,
abounding in love and faithfulness; maintaining love to thousands,
and forgiving wickedness, rebellion and sin.*

Exodus 34:6-7 NIV

Elijah, the prophet of the Most-High God, experienced the incredible
kindness and goodness of our God. In the face of his own failure, when he
ran from his assignment and sought to vindicate himself, Elijah encountered
the patience, the understanding, and the love of God! Father God does not
treat us as we deserve. It has been said, "God does not see us from our history
but from our destiny." His grace and compassion surround us.

After ten years of mission work on the field in Thailand, I was weary. Our
ambitious plans for the growth of our Thai church had not materialized.
Evangelism was difficult; many had come to the Lord only to fall away. One
day, I was having some Sabbath time with the Lord, sitting on a stone bench
on the bank of the Mekong River that flowed through the Rose Gardens,
a beautiful resort on the edge of Bangkok. I was reading the Word when I
heard the voice of the Lord in my heart, *Am I enough?*

I knew what He was asking. *Am I enough over your own desires for significance, lofty goals achieved, and recognition? Am I enough over your need for fulfillment through what you do and accomplish?*

I answered, "If I am brutally honest, no. I need more. I need to feel like I am making a difference here. I need to see fruit. I am tired of failure. I need to be 'successful' so I am validated in the eyes of our supporters back home."

Silence. I was not struck by lightning. I did not fall down dead. I, of course, knew the correct answer: He IS enough. I had to work through my disappointment. I had to get to the end of myself. My own sense of importance. Pride cannot sit on the throne of our hearts when the throne belongs to another.

James, the brother of Jesus, tells us that "Elijah was a man just like us" (James 5:17 NIV, 1984). This is an amazing statement to contemplate after reading Elijah's power encounters and miracles in the chronicles of the Kings. Elijah battled with self, with ego, and with pride. He traveled for 40 days and 40 nights until he had run out of himself. It was then that God met him on the mountain. The presence of God manifested there, not in the spectacular power of Mount Carmel, but rather in a still, small voice. In a whisper. He does not treat us as we deserve. He knows that we are flesh. His nature is good!

REFLECTION:

Who is sitting on the throne of your heart? Is it you or the Lord? How do you deal with and overcome your own pride? How do you pursue walking in humility on a daily basis?

PRAYER:

Thank you, Abba, for your incredible love and grace for us. You do not treat us as our sins deserve. Thank you that you lead us to the cross where we can be washed in the blood of the Spotless One. In your kindness, you bestow upon us sonship. Our significance is found in our relationship with you, not in our performance.

JOURNAL:

DAY 26

ELIJAH WAS A MAN JUST LIKE US

He has made everything beautiful and appropriate in its time. He has also planted eternity [a sense of divine purpose] in the human heart [a mysterious longing which nothing under the sun can satisfy, except God] — yet man cannot find out (comprehend, grasp) what God has done (His overall plan) from the beginning to the end.

Ecclesiastes 3:11 AMP

Tucked in, at the end of the book of James, are these words: "Elijah was a man just like us" (James 5:17 NIV, 1984). Startling words to us who often view the men and women of the Bible as bigger than life, superheroes, and God's chosen agents for change. Elijah was a man of flesh and blood just like us and experienced spiritual ups and downs, frustration, boredom, and breakthroughs.

What if we had a paradigm shift and saw ourselves as Father God sees us? When I was a young boy, I saw my birth announcement from the mission field and read the words my father had written: "Another hand for the harvest fields!" From a very early age I knew I had a divine purpose for my life.

God has planted greatness in us all. He has put the very DNA of Jesus into you. The God Seed. We are the very image of the Living God.

We are His representatives, not only to those living in our generation on the earth but to the spiritual forces of evil in the heavenly realms. We are called to proclaim to a dying world and live out before men, the gospel, the Good News of Jesus Christ (Mark 16:15 NIV).

REFLECTION:

Do you know who you are? Do you know your identity? Do you know that you are a son and daughter of the Living God? When you know who you are, you can walk confidently and boldly in your God-given life assignment to represent Him to the earth. We are the ambassadors of Christ
(2 Corinthians 5:20)!

PRAYER:

Father God, thank you for creating me and giving me life. Thank you for placing eternity in my heart. You said through your son King David, you stooped down to make me great (Psalm 18:35)! Thank you for making me great so that I might reflect your glory!

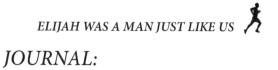

JOURNAL:

DAY 27

THE BATTLE ON THE MOUNTAIN AND IN THE VALLEY

God is my strong fortress;
And He sets the blameless in His way.
He makes my feet like hinds' feet,
And sets me on my high places.
He trains my hands for battle,
So that my arms can bend a bow of bronze.
You have also given me the shield of Your salvation,
And Your help makes me great.
You enlarge my steps under me,
And my feet have not slipped.

2 Samuel 22:33-37 NASB

On the mountain, God empowered Elijah to fight an epic battle against darkness. He wanted to show Israel that He was the God over all the earth, over all the elements. Elijah knew the power of God and had seen His work. He had prayed and no rain fell for three and a half years. He prayed and a dead boy was raised to life. He had been sustained by ravens in the wilderness and a Gentile widow in a village. In this showdown between light and darkness, God was punishing the diabolic wickedness of the gods of Baal. It was the priests of Baal that murdered the babies of Israel and offered them up as sacrifices to their gods. At the end of that saga on the mountaintop, Elijah had the priests slaughtered in the valley. They reaped what they had sown. But soon afterwards, at the threat of Jezebel the queen of the priests of Baal, Elijah runs for his life, his courage swallowed up in fear.

We often want God to remove the trial or to take us out of the battle. In Elijah's valley, God was there.

I am in this season of battling with the giant of ALS and a medical diagnosis of 3-5 years to live with no cure. I am walking in the Valley of the Shadow of Death. In this valley God is here. My battle is to trust Him, to believe His Word, to stand on His promises, to stand by faith on the Rock of Hope. I am believing for breakthrough. For a miracle. I'm believing that I will get up out of this wheelchair and walk again!

As it is written: "I have made you a father of many nations." He is our father in the sight of God, in whom he believed — the God who gives life to the dead and calls into being things that were not. Against all hope, Abraham in hope believed and so became the father of many nations, just as it had been said to him, "So shall your offspring be" (Romans 4:17-18 NIV).

Come on!

"Even though I walk through the valley of the shadow of death, I will fear no evil for you are with me" (Psalm 23:4).

And not only this, but we also exult in our tribulations, knowing that tribulation brings about perseverance; and perseverance, proven character; and proven character, hope; and HOPE [emphasis mine] does not disappoint, because the love of God has been poured out within our hearts through the Holy Spirit who was given to us. (Romans 5:3-5 NASB)

REFLECTION:

Beloved, remember the enemy will get us to focus on what God has not done yet rather than what He has done and what He is doing. Reflect on your life and determine where you are called to walk by faith. Be led by hope and anchored by His love. Today, journal the times that God has been with you on the mountaintops and in the valleys. Remember his faithfulness! He will never leave you nor forsake you! Stand on His Mighty Word! He is the faithful One!

PRAYER:

Father, thank you for walking with me in my valleys and standing with me on my mountaintops! Thank you that the best is yet ahead! Thank you that every day of life is a miracle! Thank you for answering my many prayers! Thank you for your faithfulness in the "His-story" that you have written with me. You have shown yourself faithful! I love you Abba!

JOURNAL:

Garden of the Gods in Colorado

"But the basic reality of God is plain enough. Open your eyes and there it is! By taking a long and thoughtful look at what God has created, people have always been able to see what their eyes as such can't see: eternal power, for instance, and the mystery of his divine being." Romans 1:19-20 MSG

OBEDIENCE IS GREATER THAN SACRIFICE

This is how we know that we love the children of God: by loving God and carrying out his commands. In fact, this is love for God: to keep his commands. And his commands are not burdensome, for everyone born of God overcomes the world. This is the victory that has overcome the world, even our faith.

1 John 5:2-4 NIV

In 1 Samuel, Samuel confronted King Saul and asked him, "What is this, the bleating of sheep and cattle in my ears?" (15:14). Saul's response was that he had set aside the best of the cattle for sacrifices to the Lord. Samuel then responds to Saul that the Lord had commanded him to destroy it all. Saul had not obeyed; therefore, the kingdom would be taken from him and given to a man after God's own heart.

Obedience is one of God's primary love languages. He seeks out those who are fully committed to Him. Obedience is a heart response to the will of the Father.

We train our children in obedience by telling them that the attitude of the heart is very important in how we carry out something. We train in first time obedience. We also tell our children that we as parents are seeking to obey Father God in the same way.

Fifteen years ago, my wife and I were at a conference as the senior pastor shared how they taught Kingdom obedience to their children. On a regular basis they would train their children by asking them this question, "How do we obey?"

They would respond in unison, "Quickly, cheerfully, and completely!" I was deeply impacted by what he shared and begin training our own children this way.

Elijah ran from his assignment at the threat of a tyrant, the wicked queen of Israel. After 40 days of circuitous travel, Elijah meets with God on Mount Horeb and is confronted with a question: What are you doing here, Elijah? Strange question. I thought God had called Elijah there to meet with him, but God wanted Elijah to examine his own heart, to remember his assignment, his calling, and his identity. Why was this important? The spectacular victory on Mount Carmel was at the hand of God and not man. Elijah had slipped into fear because he thought it was up to him to overcome the enemy.

The Lord will fight for you. You need only be still. Exodus 14:14

REFLECTION:

What does it look like to obey God in this season? Is there anything that God has asked you to do? What has been your response?

PRAYER:

Father, teach me daily that part of your love language is immediate obedience to you and your voice. Give me courage, discipline, and joy in walking in radical obedience to you!

JOURNAL:

DAY 29

SONSHIP

Those who are led by the Spirit of God are sons of God.

Romans 8:14 NIV, 1984

The Lord disciplines those He loves.

Hebrews 12:6

When Elijah ran for his life into the desert, God met him there. Discouraged, the wind knocked out of him, despondent and suicidal, Elijah was ready to throw in the towel. What was the Heavenly Father's response? Father God sent an angel of the Lord to feed Elijah. After resting and being fed twice, Elijah spent the next 40 days on foot working out the battle in his heart and mind. I am speculating what was going on in Elijah's heart. Why was evil still allowed to exist in Israel? Why did wickedness sit on the throne over the nation? How could fire fall from heaven, burn up the altar, and evil still be allowed to run rampant in the land? Why is God silent when so much wickedness reigns?

These are not easy questions. Does the silence of God infer that He does not care, that He's not aware? No. Embedded in the sovereignty of God is this foundational unshakeable pillar of truth: He has allowed man to have free will and to walk out the consequences of his own decisions. His heart is that all men would pursue Him and seek relationship with Him. God as our Father seeks and invites us to be a part of His family, to be His sons and daughters. True sonship is about radical obedience to the will of the Father and a heart of courage to confront the evil in our world.

Edmund Burke said this, "Evil occurs because good men do nothing."

In my own life, I am learning to take my true place as a son of the Living God and understanding my true identity as a dread warrior of the King of Kings. We as God's agents on earth are learning to confront evil and overcome it. Our elder brother Jesus learned obedience from what He suffered. Jesus was exalted to the highest place after taking up His cross and walking the path that God had appointed for Him. We are not to be those who shrink back and are destroyed but those who believe and are saved!

REFLECTION:

What is God calling you to stand for in your spheres of influence? What can you learn from the life of Elijah that will give you courage to stand for righteousness? How are you taking up your cross daily?

PRAYER:

Abba Father, would you instill in me true identity as a son and daughter of God. As a true son and a daughter, give me holy, radical, confident courage to confront evil, to advance the Kingdom of the Living God!

JOURNAL:

DAY 30

HE KNOWS
YOUR NAME

*Strengthened by that food, Elijah traveled forty days
and forty nights until he reached Horeb, the mountain of God.
There he went into a cave and spent the night.*

1 Kings 19:8 NIV

Why does God seek to meet with us on mountaintops? What is it about the heights that have a historic footprint in which we can see the presence of God?

Mount Horeb was first mentioned in Exodus chapter three when Moses was tending the sheep of Jethro, his father-in-law. This is where God appeared to Moses in a burning bush and revealed his name to him. It is also the mountain that Elijah ran to seeking the face of God. Elijah needed to encounter Him. He needed a mountaintop experience to remind him that God was indeed sovereign, all powerful, in control, and that He knew his name.

Elijah had been in a season of trial and testing. He had undergone three years of drought, of hiding in the desert, and he had endured the murders of many of his fellow prophets, his friends, by the demonic Queen Jezebel. He had just experienced tremendous spiritual warfare on another mountain, Mount Carmel, where God demonstrated the power of His mighty right hand. He showed that He was, indeed, sovereign over the false gods of the pagans that Israel had bowed to. And the word of the LORD came to him: "What are you doing here, Elijah?" (1 Kings 19:13). God called Elijah by name. He knew him. Think about this implication. We do not serve a far-off deist who created the earth and mankind and then left us to our own devices. Our God is close to us. He is personal. He is in our next breath. He knows our next thought before we think it. He knows our fears and our tears. He knows our dreams and our greatest joys. This is intimacy with our Heavenly Father. He offers us relationship and not stale religion.

In this divine dance between God and man we discover a Kingdom partnership that the Creator of the Universe offers to us. With all His sovereignty, majestic wisdom, and awesome power He has chosen to partner with mankind to advance His purposes on the earth. Stunning! We are not wooden marionettes being jerked around by some cosmic deity. We are sons and daughters of the Most-High God, and we have been given a lofty assignment: to change the world. One person at a time. One home at a time. One community at a time. One city at a time. One nation at a time. Each morning I tell my children during our morning devotional that they are world changers and history makers. Presumption? Arrogance? Not if you know your Father is the King of all kings! Not if you know your identity and your divine assignment while on Earth.

In Elijah's God encounter, there were three manifestations of the power of God displayed: wind, the earthquake, and fire. He was not in any of these. He finally spoke to Elijah in a whisper. What are you doing here, Elijah? The same question was asked again to emphasize that God wanted Elijah to think through this. It is the same question that God asked Adam and Eve in the garden after they had sinned: "Where are you?" (Genesis 3:9).

Elijah needed a paradigm shift. His lens needed to be cleaned. He needed his view of the world around him to change. The eyes of his heart needed revelation. He needed to encounter our God to regain his trust, his faith, and his hope. And at the end of the day, on that mountaintop, Elijah did have a paradigm shift when He encountered God and everything changed.

REFLECTION:

Where are you, Beloved? Have you been distant from the presence of God? Is He present within you? You are a living temple of His presence. Sometimes it takes action on our part to be restored to the place of intimacy with Him, whether it's turning from the things of this world, repenting, putting Him first, or hungering after Him. Sometimes it takes us traveling for 40 days and 40 nights to seek His face. It is worth it, and He is worth it!

PRAYER:

What an incredible revelation it is to know that the God of the universe knows my name. Thank you that you pursue me and love me. Give me a passion to share your name with all those who do not yet know you. Amen!

JOURNAL:

THE ROCK

And coming to Him as to a living stone which has been rejected by men, but is chosen and precious in the sight of God, you also, as living stones, are being built up as a spiritual house for a holy priesthood, to offer up spiritual sacrifices acceptable to God through Jesus Christ. For this is contained in Scripture: "Behold, I lay in Zion a choice stone, a precious corner stone, And he who believes in Him will not be disappointed."

1 Peter 2:4-6 NASB

Elijah, whose name means "My God is Yahweh," was a living stone in the spiritual house of Israel. He had been raised up as a prophet to hear from the Lord and speak to man. He had chosen to build his life upon a firm foundation. The rock. Jehovah God.

A few years ago, I was at a gathering of men to champion my son Kanaan's college roommate in preparation for his wedding in three weeks. We ate grilled meat, listened to some hilarious stories from their freshman and sophomore years, and then shared affirmation and advice for marriage. I shared this story from our early years on the mission field in Bangkok, Thailand:

125

We were in Thai language school our first year in the land and worked hard all week in learning a difficult and very foreign language for a western tongue. On Sundays, we took the bus downtown to a Thai congregation where we worshiped with wonderful Believers in *PraYesu*, Jesus! It was one of the highlights of our week because we were able to check our PO Box that our mail came to from the States. The PO Box was located in the basement of the nearby Indra Hotel & Shopping Complex. We soon became intrigued by a massive construction site smack in the middle of downtown, across the street from the complex. It was hidden by 20-foot walls that blocked our view from seeing inside. For months we could hear the loud noise of construction going on behind the walls. What was unusual was that we could not see any type of building going up. We were very curious. What was going on? What were they doing? Finally, after many months the building started to go up, and eventually after years of work, the tallest hotel in Southeast Asia was complete – The Baiyoke Tower II. It rose 88 stories tall like a sentinel standing proud and towering over the Bangkok skyline. I remember the day we were able to take the speed elevator to the top of the hotel to the observation deck. There we found some displays explaining how the hotel was built. I was fascinated to read that because Bangkok is below sea level and the ground not stable, the construction company had to take many months to dig down deep. They had to drive 360 massive concrete foundational pillars over 200 feet down into the earth to provide a footing strong enough to hold the massive weight of 88 floors above it.

The Lord spoke to me through this building. He reminded me of the Beatitudes and the last story of the wise and foolish builders in Matthew 7. The foolish builder threw up a beach bungalow in a matter of a few days on the warm sand and in no time was sipping lemonade, working on his tan, per modern interpretive translation. The wise builder found a location for his house that was firm and secure. A foundation that was anchored upon a mighty rock. He spent much time, sweat, and effort to forge a place of refuge where his family could live in safety. This is how we are to build our lives. We are to build our lives upon the Rock, Yeshua, the Son of the Living God. The storms of life will come, my friend. We have an adversary, Satan. He is like a roaring lion seeking many to devour. Build your house strong. Invest in your foundation. Sell all you have to buy this great treasure, this pearl of great price. Nothing compares to knowing Jesus, the Rock of Ages. Nothing compares to His immutable love.

REFLECTION:

How is the foundation of your spiritual house? What is its condition? Have you built your life and the lives of your family upon the Ancient of Days? Beloved, He is the only foundation that will stand!

PRAYER:

Thank you, Father God, that when we build our lives upon You, we have chosen a firm foundation that can never be shaken. Thank you that in the storms of life we have an anchor in you, our strong tower. Thank you that you are the Rock that has become the cornerstone of our lives. We are grateful!

JOURNAL:

DAY 32

THE SEVEN
THOUSAND

God did not reject his people, whom he foreknew. Don't you know what Scripture says in the passage about Elijah — how he appealed to God against Israel: "Lord, they have killed your prophets and torn down your altars; I am the only one left, and they are trying to kill me"? And what was God's answer to him? "I have reserved for myself seven thousand who have not bowed the knee to Baal."

Romans 11:2-4 NIV

What was it like to be a prophet like Elijah in the time of Israel?

It must have been a lonely job. God had given a message of judgment and righteousness to Elijah to speak to the king and the people of Israel. Ahab the king was furious with the message that Elijah spoke out against the wickedness of his regime. God hid Elijah in the desert for three years until the appointed time of the showdown on Mount Carmel with the prophets of Baal.

In Romans 11:2-4 listed above, we see a glimpse of Elijah's heart where he felt like he was standing alone. God's response to Elijah was this significant truth: I have 7000 that have not bowed the knee to Baal!

My wife and I were missionaries in Thailand for 16 years. Thailand is 98% Buddhist, 2% Muslim, and less than 1% Christian. The Thai people were very welcoming to us as Westerners but most were resistant to believing in and serving One God the Creator.

Sharing the gospel with an indifferent and idolatrous people can cause you to feel alone and isolated just like Elijah with the nation of Israel. Here in the West our nation is now becoming post-Christian and portions of our society are becoming antagonistic toward the gospel.

What should be our response? To stand. To stand for truth in love. "The weapons we fight with are not the weapons of the world," says Paul in 2 Corinthians 10:4. The weapons of our warfare are powerful to take down strongholds. Love. Intercession. Sharing our faith. Fasting. Worship. Gratitude. Long-suffering. Belief!

REFLECTION:

Have you ever felt alone as a believer in your workplace, school, or community? We must remember the promises of God, that he will never leave us nor forsake us! We must embrace the truth that sometimes we will be alone and feel alone. Remember that God is always with us and that he has a remnant set apart to glorify Him!

PRAYER:

Father, thank you that you have never left us nor forsaken us. Help me to remember that Elijah was a man just like us. Give us boldness and courage to stand for righteousness and truth and your Name. Help me to remember that one person and you is a majority!

JOURNAL:

DAY 33

RUNNING OUT
OF YOURSELF

Then Jesus declared, "I am the bread of life. Whoever comes to me will never go hungry, and whoever believes in me will never be thirsty."

John 6:35 NIV

After Elijah had been sustained by bread and water from the hand of the Lord, he rose from his sleep, ate again, and then traveled for 40 days and 40 nights supernaturally. What was going through the heart and mind of Elijah while he was in the desert alone? Anger? Fear? Dread? Disappointment that what he had anticipated had not materialized?

What caused him to lose heart, to lose courage, and run for his life? Elijah was grappling with many emotions. I believe God, in His infinite kindness and wisdom, allowed Elijah the time to work out the angst of his heart. I believe Elijah ran until he ran out of himself...

Humanism is a form of idolatry because it places man on the throne instead of God. Elijah found that after the spectacular victory on Mount Carmel the people were still disobedient to God. The national revival did not occur that he had so hoped for. Is it possible that somewhere along the line Elijah put himself on the throne? What if he had become filled with his own self-importance and influence and expected the people to respond dramatically in repentance to his performance on the mountain?

Pride can blind us. It keeps us from seeing our own sin and causes us to lose sight of the centrality of God on the throne. Elijah ran from his assignment. He fled the scene because he had taken his eyes off of the Father and placed them on himself. Elijah ran until he ran out of himself and ended up in the Lord's presence on Mount Horeb, the Mountain of God.

There have been times in my own life while teaching in ministry that I have shared a testimony about God working in and through me. Later, the Holy Spirit has convicted me of self-promotion. I then went back and asked for forgiveness from our staff and students. Let another praise you, and not your own mouth; someone else, and not your own lips. Proverbs 27:2

Thank you Father, for your conviction that leads us to greater freedom and peace!

REFLECTION:

What disappointments have you experienced along the road of life with God? Life is not happening as you wanted or planned? You hit a wall, a tragedy occurs, someone betrays you, and offense creeps into your heart. Take time to reflect and journal of a time that you ran from your assignment. What happened? What did you learn about yourself and about the nature of God?

PRAYER:

Father God, thank you that you accept us where we are, but you always call us up to where you are. Perspective changes everything. Thank you that you give us your eyes to see life from heaven's perspective. Thank you for your great patience and love for us as we are being transformed into your very likeness!

JOURNAL:

Red Rock Canyon in Colorado

"But the path of the righteous is like the light of dawn, That shines brighter and brighter until the full day." Proverbs 4:18 NASB

DAY 34

WHAT ARE YOU DOING HERE, ELIJAH?

Thus says the LORD, "Stand by the way and see and ask for the ancient paths, Where the good way is, and walk in it; And you will find rest for your souls."

Jeremiah 6:16 NASB

In Hebraic culture, rabbis often ask questions to influence people to think, just as Jesus asked his disciples questions to cause them to ponder and seek truth.

What are you doing here, Elijah? 1 Kings 19:13 NIV

God asked this question twice in His encounter with His prophet on Mount Horeb. Did God not know? He knew, but he wanted Elijah to examine his own heart. I believe Elijah had placed himself in the center of Israel's revival and when it did not occur, he took it personally. He was depressed. God was trying to get Elijah to raise his eyes and see past his own self-absorption, self-importance, and bitter disappointment.

I am impressed with the patience and kindness of God. He allows Elijah to work out his own failed expectations. He feeds Elijah, he allows him to rest and then to travel for 40 days in the desert to work out his raging disappointment and heartache. God does not berate Elijah but tells him to go back the way he had come and finish the assignment that God had given him.

Get back in the fight Elijah! (1 Kings 19:15).

When we fail a test or assignment, God gives us another chance to pass it, to complete our mission, to finish what He gave us to do in the first place. Repentance is humility in action. It is not simply remorse. It is obedience to the Word of the Lord, and this is love for God that we would obey His commands. Elijah's response to the Word of the Lord was to obey. He followed what God asked of him and did not shrink back this time. He returned to King Ahab's and Queen Jezebel's kingdom, to the threat of death, but this time the outcome was different.

In my own life, when the Lord asks me a question, He is asking in order for me to stop, ponder, and ask myself important questions. In Hebrews 4:11 Paul exhorts us to make every effort to enter into the rest of God. Why is this so important? It is in His rest we have time to reflect, recalibrate, and repent. True repentance leads us to greater freedom!

REFLECTION:

What assignment has the Lord given you to do? Where are you in completing this assignment? How are you walking in obedience to the Word of the Lord?

PRAYER:

Father God, thank you that you often ask me questions so that I can examine my own heart, to see where I am at in my relationship with you. Thank you that you call me out of places of complacency and passivity. Thank you that you always call me up and out to walk in your Kingdom ways. Thank you that the way of the Kingdom is not the broad and easy street but it is the Narrow Way. It is the abundant life!

JOURNAL:

DAY 35

A NEW SET OF GLASSES

I have not stopped giving thanks for you, remembering you in my prayers.
I keep asking that the God of our Lord Jesus Christ, the glorious Father,
may give you the Spirit of wisdom and revelation, so that you may know
him better. I pray that the eyes of your heart may be enlightened in order
that you may know the hope to which he has called you,
the riches of his glorious inheritance in his holy people,
and his incomparably great power for us who believe.

Ephesians 1:16-19a NIV

I've heard it said, we overcome adversity when we take our eyes off the problem and focus on The Problem Solver. Elijah had a vision problem. He was focused on the wrong thing. When we are focused on the wrong thing we end up in the desert. We end up traveling for many days "trying to find our glasses" – forty in this case.

In the Bible, forty represents a season of testing. Scholars say that Mount Horeb was only a 9-11-day journey from the broom tree near Beersheva where Elijah started his journey. Why did it take him 40 days? I believe he had to work out his disappointment and recalibrate. He had to come to the end of his own self and resources. Self-reliance is another word for independence. Independence can be dangerous when it leads to rebellion. Lucifer was cast down out of heaven because he no longer wanted to submit to God. He wanted to be equal with God.

It is stunning that God would choose man to partner with, to work His purposes on the earth. God used a man, Elijah, to represent Himself to Israel. Elijah was not a perfect man; he was just like us. Elijah had to work out his own perceptions, expectations, and demands of God before he could be used for the next assignment. God, you alone are sovereign!

I found in my own life that when I have a spiritual vision problem it is because I am self-focused and not God-focused. When I focus on myself, my problems are bigger than my reality. When I focus on God, my problems become much smaller. They are put into proper perspective. It is what is called a paradigm shift.

REFLECTION:

What set of glasses are you currently using to view your life? How have you been intentional in wearing Kingdom glasses and not the glasses of the world? What recent paradigm shifts have you gone through by putting on the King's glasses?

PRAYER:

Abba Father, through your great grace and big heart would you give me your eyes to see the world, not my own. Help me to see the world and my fellowman with your eyes of compassion and grace. Thank you for your incredible love and kindness that you would open up the eyes of my heart!

JOURNAL:

FAITHFULNESS

However, when the Son of Man comes, will he find faith on the earth?

Luke 18:8b NIV

Elijah was a man of great faith. He stood as one man against hundreds of false prophets and before Israel, a people that were hardened by idolatry, sin, and rebellion. One of Elijah's exemplary models came from the biblical patriarch Abraham who is known as the Father of our Faith.

We often speak about the faith of Abraham, the father of faith to both Jew and Gentile. Faith is a big deal to God. In fact, Hebrews 11:6 says that without faith it is impossible to please God. It is the currency of heaven and it is what moves the Kingdom on earth. It has been said that nothing, absolutely nothing, happens in the Kingdom without faith. What did Abraham possess that his contemporaries did not? He had the ability to believe what was not yet. Abraham trusted the Word of God, the promises of God more than the immediate experience around him. He set his eyes not on what was seen, but what was unseen. For "what is seen is temporary but what is unseen is eternal" (2 Corinthians 4:18).

Did Abraham do this perfectly? No. He followed the counsel of Sarah and slept with her handmaiden, Hagar, and saw Ishmael born. This was not God's chosen seed. God still blessed Ishmael and his line. They are a numerous people group in the Middle East today. Abraham still had to wait and trust. It was not until over 20 years after the promise given to Abraham that Isaac was born.

In my own life, I have been called to walk in faith when our son Isaiah was born and was not breathing. The Lord had given us the name Isaiah in a dream to my wife Samantha early on in the pregnancy. Isaiah means "Jehovah Saves." At that moment in the hospital delivery room, when there was no breath coming out of Isaiah's mouth, we prophesied life over him, "Jehovah saves, Jehovah saves!" Today, 18 years later, Isaiah is in his freshman year in college and we see God at work in his life.

Do you want the faith of Abraham and Elijah? Do you want to walk as a man or woman of great faith? Believe. John says that the work of God is to believe in the One whom God has sent (John 6:29). In our western culture, faith is a noun but in Hebrew culture it is an action verb. It is not merely intellectual consent but rather a lifestyle of action. It moves us to act and change and believe.

REFLECTION:

What promise are you standing on at this hour? What in your life right now requires faith to believe for? Journal times in your life when faith was required for you to move forward. If we lack faith we can ask for more! (James 1:5-8).

PRAYER:

Thank you Father, that you call us to be men and women of faith. To believe you at your Word. Thank you that you have built history with us that confirms your Word and promises in our life. Stretch us, O God! Increase our faith to believe you for the unseen, miracles, and the not yet.

JOURNAL:

DAY 37

AN UPSIDE-DOWN KINGDOM

Then he said to them all: "Whoever wants to be my disciple must deny themselves and take up their cross daily and follow me. For whoever wants to save their life will lose it, but whoever loses their life for me will save it."

Luke 9:23-24 NIV

God called Elijah to stand on the face of Mount Horeb. To stand in His presence, where He proceeded to demonstrate His raw power before him. A violent tornado blasted the side of the mountain, tearing it apart and showering rocks. I'm certain that Elijah was terrified, wondering if this would be the day he would die. But the Lord was not in the tornado. Then an earthquake shook the mountain, rocking it to its core. But the Lord was not in the earthquake. Then fire scorched the top of the mountain, blackening the rocks. But the Lord was not in the fire. Finally, there came a gentle whisper, the voice of God.

DAY 37

We live in an upside-down Kingdom. If we come into His Kingdom with the eyes of the world, we will miss our visitation.

We expect a powerful demonstration of the power of God and He comes in a gentle whisper. We expect to be delivered by a Warrior King and He comes as a fragile, innocent baby born in a common stable and not in the upper echelons of the powerful, rich, and elite.

I believe he demonstrated His power to Elijah again for the second time on Mount Horeb as he had done on Mount Carmel to show Elijah His changing ways. How? The first time he showed Elijah His power. The second time he showed Elijah intimacy through His gentle whisper.

In my own life, I am on a lifelong quest of learning the ways of God. I have become aware that His ways change all the time so that we do not depend on a formula but rather upon the very presence and person of God.

I have spent many years in my life pursuing servant leadership, the highest form of leadership in the Kingdom. I failed as many times as I succeeded in the earlier years. One mentor calls it descending into greatness. Going lower still. I must die to self, relinquish self-ego and pride to take hold of something that is worth infinitely greater, the humility of Christ. It's only when I walk in humility that I will receive wisdom, spiritual discernment, and understand His nature.

I remember vividly back in 1996 on the mission field receiving the baptism of the Holy Spirit and becoming excited about opportunities to grow in evangelism with the Thai people. Soon afterwards we were back in the United States on a furlough and I received a prophetic word that humbled me. I was expecting and hoping for a lofty prophetic word that would have me speaking before thousands. Instead this pastor said they saw me stacking chairs. It finally dawned on me that Father God is more interested in building my character than my resumé! Welcome to the upside-down Kingdom!

REFLECTION:

Describe in your own words the upside-down Kingdom of Jesus. How have you learned to walk in this Kingdom? What empowers you to do this on a daily basis?

PRAYER:

Thank you, Father for introducing me to the upside-down Kingdom. Your ways are higher than our ways. Thank you that you never call us to something that you did not first walk in and model for us. Thank you that everything in the Kingdom is done in your power and not ours.

JOURNAL:

DAY 38

THEY WILL RUN AND NOT GROW WEARY

Why do you say, O Jacob, and complain, O Israel, "My way is hidden
from the LORD; my cause is disregarded by my God"?
Do you not know? Have you not heard?
The Lord is the everlasting God, the Creator of the ends of the earth.
He will not grow tired or weary, and his understanding no one can fathom.
He gives strength to the weary and increases the power of the weak.
Even youths grow tired and weary, and young men stumble and fall; but
those who hope in the Lord will renew their strength.
They will soar on wings like eagles; they will run and not grow weary,
they will walk and not be faint.

Isaiah 40:27-31 NIV

In the story of Elijah, after he sees the awesome power of God displayed
before the nation of Israel, on top of Mount Carmel, he runs for his life in

utter despondency, under the crushing weight of a death warrant from the wicked Queen Jezebel.

In the wilderness for 40 days, Elijah is alone with his thoughts and the sovereignty of God. Sometimes God has to take us out of the heat of battle, out of the fray so that we can recalibrate and refocus on what is most important.

I have been on my own "40 days in the wilderness journey" while battling ALS. What have I learned on my journey? God is faithful even in the midst of monumental disappointments as I have lost the ability to walk or to raise my arms. I have seen the faithfulness of God through opportunities to continue to minister and serve others through teaching, training, fathering, mentoring, and leadership coaching. He has supplied our every need as a family.

At times, disappointment over unanswered prayer weighs heavily on my spirit. Hope deferred threatens to topple me. Focused solely upon my circumstances, I could be sucked into a vortex of discouragement and depression. At times, suicidal thoughts flicker on the horizon of my thought life just as Elijah battled with chest-squeezing depression in the desert and wanted to die. How do we overcome the attacks of the enemy?

We take up the Sword of the Spirit, the mighty, double-edged Word of God in our hands. Read again, at the top, the scripture, the rallying anthem cry of Isaiah as He trumpets truth over our circumstances.

REFLECTION:

Are you presently battling with depression or discouragement? Hope in the Lord! Take up the Word of God and wield it as a mighty sword against the attacks of the enemy. He will renew your strength and restore you! Journal how the Lord has led you through dark valleys and over obstacles to overcome the enemy.

PRAYER:

Father God, thank you for sustaining me through many trials and valleys. You are the lifter of our heads! You are the giver of all good gifts! You are the hope restorer! Thank you for giving me wings to soar like an eagle!

JOURNAL:

DAY 39

BURN THE PLOW

So Elijah went from there and found Elisha son of Shaphat. He was plowing with twelve yoke of oxen, and he himself was driving the twelfth pair. Elijah went up to him and threw his cloak around him. Elisha then left his oxen and ran after Elijah. "Let me kiss my father and mother goodbye," he said, "and then I will come with you."
"Go back," Elijah replied. "What have I done to you?"
So Elisha left him and went back. He took his yoke of oxen and slaughtered them. He burned the plowing equipment to cook the meat and gave it to the people, and they ate. Then he set out to follow Elijah and became his servant.

1 Kings 19:19-21 NIV

"When God calls a man, He calls that man to die."

Dietrich Bonhoeffer

(Theologian, Pastor, Spy, and Martyr in World War II.)

DAY 39

What does it cost to be a disciple of Jesus?

Everything.

When Elijah called Elisha to follow him, Elisha made the necessary steps to set his face like flint and not turn back. He willingly slaughtered his oxen as a free will offering to the Lord and burned the plow. At what cost? What were oxen worth in that day? A significant sum. The story of Elisha leaving everything behind to follow the prophet Elijah reminds me of a story from the 15th century. Hernán-Cortés arrived in the New World with 600 men and immediately ordered his men to destroy the ships. He wanted to make it abundantly clear that there was no turning back on their conquest. Cortés stands as a tremendous example of leadership and sacrifice.

In my youth, I was a part of our high school tennis team in Atlanta, Georgia. I played because I wanted to be like my older brother David. I remember one day after a long practice my brother and I were walking to the car talking about life. We talked about how many years it would take to become a professional tennis player. We both looked at each other and smiled. My brother said, "Fame and wealth pale in comparison to the honor and privilege of serving God for the rest of my life." He went on to marry in his mid 20's. He and his wife were living the "American Dream" pulling down six-figure incomes in very good jobs in Dallas, Texas. They left it all to become missionaries in Northern Thailand for 25 years during which time David almost died of a tropical disease. They had burned the plow.

Foxe's Book of Martyrs records the death of the disciples of Jesus. With the exceptions of John, who was exiled to the Island of Patmos in the book of Revelation, and Judas, who betrayed Jesus, all were martyred for following Jesus. They did not love their lives so much as to shrink from death.[1]

---

[1] The *Actes and Monuments*, popularly known as *Foxe's Book of Martyrs*, is a work of Protestant history and martyrology by Protestant English historian John Foxe, first published in 1563 by John Day.

REFLECTION:

What would you burn your plow for? In Matthew 13:45-46, Jesus said the Kingdom of God was like a merchant who sold everything to buy the pearl of great price. What are you willing to give for His kingdom?

PRAYER:

Father God, thank you that you laid down your life for us and set an example for how we are to live our lives. Thank you that it is by your power that we live and not by our own strength. Thank you that we are living not for this life but for eternity! We praise you that you're worthy of giving our all for your Name!

JOURNAL:

Garden of the Gods in Colorado

"The Lord loves seeing justice on the earth. Anywhere and everywhere you can find his faithful, unfailing love!" Psalm 33:5 TPT

DAY 40

CHARIOTS OF FIRE

As they were walking along and talking together, suddenly a chariot of fire and horses of fire appeared and separated the two of them, and Elijah went up to heaven in a whirlwind. Elisha saw this and cried out, "My father! My father! The chariots and horsemen of Israel!" And Elisha saw him no more. Then he took hold of his garment and tore it in two.

2 Kings 2:11-12 NIV

When you think of the life of Elijah, this scene from 2 Kings 2 is one of the most impactful and significant. The Lord tells Elisha that his master would be taken that day. Elisha, who has served Elijah faithfully, wants to be present when Elijah is taken to heaven. Three times Elijah moves to a different location in Central Israel. From Bethel to Jericho to the Jordan River. Three times Elisha asks to go with Elijah. Elijah asks Elisha if there's anything that he wants before he goes. Elisha could have asked this Man of God for riches or fame but instead he asks for a double portion.

In the language of the Hebrew culture, he was asking for a double portion of inheritance that the firstborn son would ask of his father. No longer the servant of Elijah, but a spiritual son, Elisha is stepping into his full inheritance as the successor of Elijah, becoming the next prophet of God for Israel. Elisha indeed received a double portion because he goes on to perform twice as many miracles as Elijah did.

The supernatural appearance of the chariots of fire also profoundly shows the amazing intimacy and honor that was placed upon Elijah that he did not have to pass through the veil of death to meet our Maker. God sent a heavenly escort to usher him into the gates of heaven. What an incredible honor!

We have come to the end of this 40-day journey together. Thank you for investing your time, focus, and heart into this spiritual journey. I pray that the past 40 days have been impactful in your life. Jesus said in the Beatitudes that those who hunger and thirst for righteousness will be filled. May this journey produce great spiritual fruit in your life, and a greater appreciation for the presence of the Lord, the nature of God, and the love of the Father for us.

As I close this devotional journey on this 40th day, I leave you with these thoughts from Henry David Thoreau: "The mass of men lead lives of quiet desperation." What a sobering statement. As Believers, we are indebted to the Lord for saving us from darkness, despair, and desperation. I challenge you to live a life that is worthy of our King! Every day, may you reflect the love and heart of the Father to those around you.

In my own personal journey, the past five years of being in this fiery crucible of testing, I've learned the ever closeness of my Heavenly Father. He is Emanuel, God with us! He will never leave nor forsake us!

There have been many lessons that I have been growing in over these past few years. Learning to walk in greater humility. Growing in patience. Forgiving others with the same great grace that has been shown to me by Father God.

Possessing a greater measure of faith for healing breakthrough. Taking hold of the tenacious belief that the One who spoke the stars into existence is my Healer and can heal me.

Maranatha! Come Lord Jesus! To you belong all praise, glory, and honor! You're worthy of the adoration of all the generations. We adore you Father God! We worship you!

Come!

Steve Allen
October 19, 2019

APPENDIX:

What I see in the life of Stephen Chesshir Allen, is a man who runs after God's promises.

And He Ran for 40 Days is a challenge to live and run like no other. Beyond our view of any pain and suffering from the heat we are in, we keep our eyes on the goal and we keep our faith in Him. We were born to run... and we were born to live forever. Steve Allen is running his race to win. Instead of living in desperation, every page of this devotional brings inspiration to all who long for a glorious outcome.

Rand Chesshir
November 17th, 2019
Salem, Oregon

This song is a tribute to the Thai Mission Team who served many years together in Bangkok, Thailand. Thank you for impacting my life and inspiring me to run after Jesus.

Steve & Tina Countrymen
Tim & Sherry Walter
Russ & Tracy Pennington
Steve & Samantha Allen

THE IMPOSSIBLE DREAM

To dream the impossible dream
To fight the unbeatable foe
To bear with unbearable sorrow
To run where the brave dare not go

To right the unrightable wrong
To love pure and chaste from afar
To try when your arms are too weary
To reach the unreachable star

This is my quest, to follow that star
No matter how hopeless, no matter how far
To fight for the right
Without question or pause

To be willing to march
Into hell for a heavenly cause
And I know if I'll only be true
To this glorious quest

That my heart will lay peaceful and calm
When I'm laid to my rest
And the world will be better for this

That one man scorned and covered with scars
Still strove with his last ounce of courage
To fight the unbeatable foe
To reach the unreachable star

"The Impossible Dream (The Quest)" is a popular song composed by Mitch Leigh, with lyrics written by Joe Darion. The song is the most popular song from the 1965 Broadway musical Man of La Mancha and is also featured in the 1972 film of the same name starring Peter O'Toole.

SEVEN KINGDOM TREASURES
FROM THE LIFE OF ELIJAH

1 - SEEK HIS FACE!

Elijah was hidden in a desert valley for three years.
1 Kings 17:1-6 ~ Psalm 27:4 ~ Psalm 91:1 ~ Mark 1:35

2 - RAISE THE DEAD!

God raises the Zarephath widow's son from the dead.
1 Kings 17:17-24 ~ Matthew 10:7-8

3 - STAND FOR RIGHTEOUSNESS!

Elijah stands as the lone prophet against the 450 prophets of Baal.
1 Kings 18:16-46 ~ Ephesians 6:13-14

4 - WHEN YOU STUMBLE GET BACK UP!

Terrified and exhausted, Elijah runs for his life after receiving the news of
Queen Jezebel's death warrant on his head.
1 Kings 19:1-4 ~ Proverbs 24:16 ~ 1 Corinthians 10:12-13

5 - ENDURE THE TEST!

After fleeing from the enemy Elijah travels for 40 days to the
mountain of God. Forty represents testing in the Bible.
1 Kings 19:5-8 ~ Hebrews 10:35-39 ~ Hebrews 12:1-3

6 - MEET HIM ON THE MOUNTAIN!

Elijah stands before the presence of the Lord.
1 Kings 19:9-18 ~ Psalm 15 ~ Psalm 24 ~ Psalm 121

7 - PASS THE MANTLE!

Elijah passes off his mantle to Elisha.
We are to raise up the next generation.
1 Kings 19:19 ~ Psalm 78:1-7 ~ 2 Timothy 2:2

NOTE FROM AUTHOR:

Most of these names you have never heard of. They are known by me. I count it a high privilege and honor to know these men and women of God. They have walked with me for many years, some of them decades. I am humbled to have been blessed and impacted by each one of them. They have changed my life.

Grateful!

Steve Allen

Steve Allen is a man of the highest integrity and honor, a true disciple of Christ. He lives his life leaning on the truths of God's Word. When you enter into the pages of *And He Ran for 40 Days*, you enter into an intimate journey with a man facing the greatest challenges of his life and yet finding the closeness of the Father at every turn. Get ready to experience God in a deep and powerful way.

Paul Amabile
President Amabile Ministries International

Steve Allen's friendship has changed the course of our family's life through his quiet but powerful devotion to the Lord and his tender way with all those he walks with. Steve showed us, through example, how to really put others first and now in the midst of his greatest life challenge he is choosing to selflessly share his faith and hope in this unique and anointed devotional.

Leonardo and Una Bella
Founders of Israel Prayer Mission

In the book of James, it says that blessed is the man who remains steadfast under trial for he shall receive the crown of life God has promised those that love Him (1:12). I don't know that I have ever met a man under such intense trials as Steve who continually diffuses the fragrance of the knowledge of Christ wherever he goes. Steve has been commissioned by the Lord to inspire leaders and raise up thousands upon thousands of sons who one day will be true Fathers in the Spirit. Steve has devoted himself to family, prayer, and the ministry of the word and this 40-day devotional journal reflects his amazing journey into Christ. This journal is filled with revelation, practical application, and teaching that inspires us to believe again that with God, nothing is impossible. In love, respect, and admiration I wholeheartedly endorse this man and his writing.

Chris Berglund
Senior Leader of The Call
Founder Ascending Zion Ministries

As a father, mentor, and champion to this generation, Steve's life is a testimony of great courage and enduring faith! He is a beacon light to the goodness of God even in the darkest night. This 40-day devotional journey is not only inspiring but will impact and challenge you to live a life worthy of the King of all kings!

Geri Bridston
Teacher, Discipler, Artist
Mother and Grandmother

I have had the privilege of previewing Steve Allen's *And He Ran for 40 Days* devotional. You don't have to be in a deep valley like Steve to be lifted up by these prophetic devotions. They are each filled with profound encouragement, heavenly reflections for Steve's journey, and Holy Spirit encounters and conviction.

Dr. Jay Capra, M.D.
Husband, father, grandfather, pediatrician, mentor to men and a thankful recipient of Steve's Leadership Coaching for the past 4 years.

James 5:17 says that "Elijah was a man just like us." The Kingdom principles in this book that Steve has learned from Elijah's life have helped him persevere for years in the midst of one of the most difficult diagnoses. I believe these principles have the potential to likewise strengthen you to run in the midst of your own journey and hardships.

Michael Allen
Training School Coordinator
Contend Global

When you think about how God speaks to man in the present, we know He speaks to us through His Son. Stephen Chesshir Allen is a man who speaks what he hears from God. *And He Ran for 40 Days* captures what the Lord is saying through a man whose faith has changed the lives of countless souls in the pursuit of life's greatest goal...to know and be known by our heavenly Father.

Randall Stephen Chesshir
Chairman L. Haskell Chesshir Foundation

And He Ran for 40 Days is an epic journey into living more closely with God in the midst of challenges that supersede human understanding. Steve shares how God enables victory in our lives in spite of monumental life struggles and challenges. Prepare to 'run' a race with Steve that will delightfully draw you closer to God's heart in your own race.

Rogers Clayton
CEO of Korban Investments

ENDORSEMENTS

My friend, Steve, is His precious child as am I, and we will trust our King to protect us and lead us through every trial. I have seen in my dreams, Steve, hopping out of bed with surprise and overwhelming joy in the face of his miraculous healing. God is always good as well as mysterious beyond all measure. "Your will be done, on Earth as it is in heaven..." Matthew 6:10

Johnny d'Artenay
Jesus Follower, Family Man, Musician
Nashville, TN

I have known Steve for ten years and I have seen up close how he is a loving husband, father, friend, and mentor. If there was one word that would describe Steve, it would be "integrity". Steve is one of the most upstanding men I have ever met and someone that I have placed the highest value on as a friend. I can assure you that you will find wisdom, encouragement, and hope as you read this book and you will discover God's voice speaking to you as Steve unpacks his journey with God and the "Life" he discovers as he walks with his best Friend.

Jeff Dollar
Senior Pastor Grace Center
Author of *Letting Go of the Need to Be Right*

This is not a devotional book — this is a discipleship book. Steve's insights and reflection questions helped me discover fears and limiting beliefs that were holding me back, and to resolve to live God's best for my life.

Ben DuBose
Owner
1242 Property Investments, LLC

I have had the honor of being coached and mentored by Steve Allen for over 10 years; from personal experience I can attest that Steve Allen is a formidable man of God. The pages of this book contain deep wisdom and truth that come from a lifetime of faithfully walking with Jesus.

Alex Eagle
Vice President
Eagle Permian Partners, LLC

From a missionary and a mentor, from a father and a friend, from a builder and a brother, from a saint who has suffered, comes a forty-day feast of a lifetime of wisdom, the Word, and wonder. Fast for forty days and eat a meal a day with this bread from heaven and you will grow strong in spirit – or simply enjoy this daily manna when you walk with God in cool of the Garden. Then like Steve Allen, a true Elijah father in this generation, you'll hear the still small voice of God and receive a fresh commission from the Father.

Lou Engle
Visionary Co-founder of The Call
Author of The Jesus Fast

When writing about Steve Allen, I will never be able to find the words to describe this amazing man of God. He is a living example of how to walk through a turbulent life situation, in his case the worst kind of medical diagnosis, and never lose step with Jesus. He is the Encourager of all encouragers, constantly speaking life from a place of not yet having seen the full victory, but confident of the outcome. Walk with him and be challenged to follow him as he follows Jesus.

Don Finto
Pastor Emeritus of Belmont Church and founder of the Caleb Company
Author of *Your People Shall Be My People*, *God's Promise and the Future of Israel*, and *The Handbook for the End Times*

We tend to write about heroes once their grand feats have been accomplished. Steve is a true hero to me. Already outstanding in his life and personal history, his greatest feats have been his daily choices in the face of daunting and ongoing odds before which he refuses to bow. His internal devotion and holy, determined discipline have equipped him with the tenacity of an Olympic long-distance runner. If I'm looking for encouragement, I just listen to Steve. Regardless of the subject, Jesus and His ways will shine brightly, because in Him, Steve lives and moves and has his being. In Steve's life we see made tangible that intangible substance called faith. Anyone looking for a true hero, read on.

Dave Fitzpatrick
Executive Director
The Institute for Cross Cultural Affairs

This devotional book is a rich look at the trials and testing of Elijah through the eyes of my friend, Steve Allen. I do not know anyone else who could reveal this journey to us the way he has. He was chosen for it. *And He Ran for 40 Days* will present you with the rewards of Steve's own personal race, by way of his remarkable tenacity and strength.

Grahm Foster
Teaching staff Contend Global
Photographer, writer, wood craftsman, husband, and father

Steve Allen has done it again! This book is an excellent way to glean from one of the most godly fathers I have ever met. I am confident this book will give you a tremendous amount of wisdom and practical ways to further your intimacy with the Lord Jesus Christ. There is no one I'd rather have lead me to greater depths of leadership than Steve Allen!

Zachary Garza Sr.
Founder and Executive Director of Forerunner Mentoring Program
Founder of You Can Mentor

ENDORSEMENTS

So rich!! Like eating a box of Godiva chocolates! You will drink deeply from the well of Steve's unwavering faith. His challenging journey with ALS will draw you to the heart of God. This mighty man of God's journey of faith has impacted my life like none other. His collection of life experiences paralleled with Elijah will definitely advance the Kingdom.

Dr. Jerry Gooch – Heart Surgeon
Carol Gooch – Women's Discipleship Leader
Father & Mother of 3, Grandparents of 9
Memphis, Tennessee

There is no one I know who walks straighter and with more strength than my friend Steve Allen. In this journal and reflection testimony, Steve lays out scripture and thoughts on how you can walk up any mountain or obstacle in your life with God's providential hand. Steve has blessed my life and this book will do the same for you.

Lawrence Goodwyn
English/Bible Teacher
Middle Tennessee Christian School

Steve Allen's 40-day devotional *And He Ran for 40 Days* is a must read, because it's going to boost your faith to overcome! When I was reading it, I literally could not put it down, as I was so encouraged. Honestly, it is anointed. I was so inspired by Steve's testimony of faith, despite his personal battle with ALS. He puts his trust in YESHUA THE HEALER by overcoming the giant Goliath like David did – speaking what God says to the mountain of impossibility to be cast out into the sea by praising and thanking Emmanuel. God who is with us and who fights our battles! He is a man of faith like the heroes of faith in the book of Hebrews; as an Abraham who believed in God and it was credited to him as righteousness, he received his promised son Isaac! Like Job the righteous man of God whose faith was tested and the test turned to testimony of his healing and redemption by the Redeemer Who Lives, Who brought Resurrection life to the Valley of dry bones and he received double for all his trouble! He is a Father to the Nations as an Elijah who is turning the hearts of children to the Heavenly Father, by the way he is running the race and not quitting but winning the PRIZE fixing his eyes on the Author and Finisher of our Faith, who will reward his faith and will not die but live and declare the glory of the LORD!

Samaa Habib
Author of *Face to Face with Jesus*

Steve lives what he writes, and he calls us to a ruthless trust in our Heavenly Father while being tested by fire. He challenges us to rise and face the evil of our day, to live lives worthy of our Lord, fulfilling our destinies, while believing that Jesus is worthy of it all.

Kendall Hewitt
Executive Director
Firestoke, Inc.

Steve Allen is one of my heroes of the faith. I am grateful and honored to call him friend and for the opportunity to minister together in a life group, for which he was the leader. I've witnessed the powerful impact Steve has had equipping leaders and impacting nations. Steve lives out his faith with obedience, love and grace, willing to invest in everyone and anyone. *And He Ran for 40 Days* is a modern day *My Utmost for His Highest*. It inspires and exhorts with love and courage through a life whose hope and source is an intimate daily encounter with Jesus – the Living Word.

Loren Johnson
Founder and CEO Christopher Entertainment Organization
Music Entrepreneur/Worship Leader

Having the privilege of having known and shared life with Steve Allen here in Colorado Springs with the Contend Movement, we are so excited that this book is finally being released. Steve is an embodiment of a "living epistle," a true father in the spirit and faithful son of God. As leaders and as a community we can testify that his life has already marked and been "written in" our hearts. Here at last he can be "known and read by all," and the world is better for it. Thank you, Steve for being a world-changer and a history-maker!

David and Audry Kim
Directors of Contend Global

Jesus promised us that we would experience trials and tribulations throughout our lives. Facing this reality is something that the church in America today is poorly equipped to handle. When reading *And He Ran for 40 Days* you will be both encouraged and strengthened by the power of my dad's personal testimony as well as the biblical precedents put forth on how to walk through your wilderness season. This is a must read!

Kanaan Allen
Training School Coordinator
Contend Global

Steve Allen is in a unique position to write this excellent devotional as he's been challenged like few of us ever will. Yet despite his now five-year struggle with ALS, he has proven that nothing can keep him from his commitment to Jesus. He has responded to his circumstances with supernatural faith, incredible resolve, and a devotion to his Creator that demonstrates for all to see and emulate, the unmistakable character of the "man of God" he was made to be.

Chris Mandel
President, Excellence in Risk Management, LLC
Business executive, follower of Jesus, husband, father, and grandfather

ENDORSEMENTS

And He Ran for 40 Days is a wonderful blending of the word of God, the ways of God, and the prophetic purposes of God. Little-known biblical facts are insightfully woven into the daily portions, enriching the reader's understanding of the Jewish times and culture. This devotional has the unique component of Steve's journey with ALS. He gives us a very personal view of his own journey encountering the loss of physical abilities, while experiencing increase in relational intimacy with Father, Son, and Holy Spirit.

Dabney Mann
Founder and President of MercyMoves

And He Ran for 40 Days is a devotional for the man or woman of God who is serious about their walk with the Lord. It imparts hope and courage for the journey of life. Using the Scriptures, biblical characters and events, the writer invites the reader to view life as mountains to be climbed, and races to be run, while encountering God and His purposes along with great obstacles to be overcome. It is replete with little-known biblical facts, Hebraic insights, and traditions. I was greatly enriched by this timely book.

Doug Mann
Marketplace Evangelist

I have known Steve Allen since he was a child living with his missionary parents in Korea. He served with our ministry in Bangladesh and I have known him to be a faithful man in every aspect of those two words, both faithful and a real man. He is highly disciplined physically and in his dedication to God and to his family. Steve's battle with ALS has proven his faith to be gold. He keeps his eyes focused on Jesus and never gives up. I have yet to find him depressed or discouraged. You'll be blessed by this book as Steve shares his pathway to holding Jesus high and lifted up in his heart and life.

Dwight Marable
President, Missions International
Author of *Motivation for Mission* and *Natural Evangelism*

Stephen Allen has walked faithfully with the Lord for many decades, experiencing great mountaintop victories as well as going through dark valleys. Through it all he has learned what it is to be content in the arms of Jesus. This 40-day devotional can help each one of us to take courage for the long journey.

David Allen
Consultant for Mission Resource Network

The weight of this book is the genuine reflection of Christ in the author. Steve is a rare individual who walks the talk of his relationship with Christ in every aspect of his life. The fruit of that walk has touched all of us who have the privilege of knowing him. Walk with him through the pages and I know it will be life-changing for you.

Rev. Joan Masterson
Founder One in Messiah Ministries

At freshmen college orientation, I "accidentally" came into contact with Steve Allen. By the Father's gracious providence, he became my roommate that first year into my adulthood. More importantly, he became my friend. Since that time, Steve's life and friendship have spurred me to love Jesus like few others the Father has put into my path. And now I have watched with awe this most recent season as he has battled with courage and a never-wavering faith, a disease that is ravaging his physical body. If anyone has the authority to speak to us about running our race with the strength of the Lord when we feel weak, it is this man. I can't encourage you enough to not merely purchase this book but to go on a 40-day journey with Steve. My almost four decades of friendship testify – you will come out much stronger on the other side.

David McQueen
Lead Pastor
Beltway Park Church, Abilene, TX

Enter into this 40-day journey of prayer, revelation, reflection, and praise as Steve leads us to the mountains and through the valleys. Scripture comes alive as you run with Elijah and Steve, are guided by the Word to battle interior foes, and receive strength and healing from angelic hosts. ALS seeks to overtake this courageous man of God but he will not be stopped. Steve has been my mentor and coach during this time and God has profoundly used him to take me deeper into God's heart and purposes for my life. Come along with this prophetic leader. You will be blessed.

Martha Monnett, MPH, M.Div.
Minister, Evangelist, Mother, Grandmother

I am greatly encouraged by this devotional drawn from the lives of the prophet Elijah, and the man of God, Steve Allen, forged in the refining fires of adversity, tempered by God's enduring love and faithfulness. I've only read about Elijah, but I know Steve personally and some of his battle against ALS. Never have I heard him complain or grumble through this challenge...my ears have only heard the high praises for the Most-High God come from his mouth. Steve is a real-life inspiration to me and many others, spurring us on to faithfully run our own races, and I highly recommend this 40-day devotional.

Hugh Nemets
Author of *Dead Jew Walking: A Jewish Man's Journey from Death to Life*

Steve is a disciple maker who embodies the words servant leader probably more than any man I know. Watching Steve persevere in faith through the difficulty and suffering of this season of his life has been an example to myself and many others. I can think of no other man qualified to deal with the theme outlined in this devotional than he is. His words "the truth is greater than the facts we face" should challenge all of us to take an eternal view of life. This devotional based on Elijah's life will challenge you to ascend the mountain of the Lord, to stand fast on God's Word, encourage you to pour out your heart to Him in the valley, and finally to fight the good fight of faith and finish well. Thank you, Steve, for this timely and important contribution to the Kingdom of God.

Michael Niebur
Team Leader Derech Avraham
Jerusalem, Israel

ENDORSEMENTS

Through serving the Lord together 16 years in Thailand, Steve Allen became my closest friend and confidant. I have watched Steve battle ALS for the past five years and questioned why a man of God like Steve would suffer so intensely. As I devoured this book, I realized that the lessons he has learned are going to be life-giving to many who are in the midst of a fiery trial. They have been forged and purified in the fire, and they are of more value than pure gold!

Russ Pennington
Director Bethesda Outreach Center

We were amazed and challenged by this devotional to go deeper with God and to journal with Him as we went in-depth to hear what God was saying. Most of all, to hear through Steve's own words how God's love, hope, and faithfulness over the last five years as he has battled ALS, has given him a supernatural insight into the heart of God!

Mike and Sisse Pfieffer
Elders at Grace Center, Franklin, TN

Steve is one of the most intentional people I know. While serving with him I have seen him demonstrate the attributes and character of the Father, bringing hope to the lost and strength to the body of Christ. As you join Steve in his journey through this devotional, prepare your heart to encounter the Living God.

David Pickman
Automation Nth
VP of Operations
Prayer Partner, Dad

You give people what you are, not what you say. This phrase is evident in Steve Allen's *And He Ran for 40 Days* where you will find encouragement and challenge to run your race through Steve's own courageous battle with ALS and his unwavering faith.

Jon Pinkston
Businessman

This 40-day reading is a powerful look into the faithfulness of Abba in situations that can feel hopeless. I highly recommend this book as a deep perspective changer!

David Shore
President
Green Pastures Landscape Company

Full of scripture and truth. It's wonderful to be spurred on in my own spiritual race by one of the greatest spiritual runners.

Cody Weeks
Sculptor, real estate investor, husband and father

Forty days or years was a period of time God often used to test and work out things in the lives of His people. He used it to produce what was needed to carry out His plans and purposes. You are embarking on a 40-day journey that will do the same. Steve is a faithful, trusted, and battle-tested husband, father, friend, and passionate follower of Jesus. His experiences and unwavering reliance on the truth and power of God's Word will help reignite you in courageous obedience to God's purposes and plans for your life.

Brett Whitley
Senior Wealth Advisor – Ronald Blue Trust
Father, husband, friend, follower of Jesus

I have had the immense honor of walking with Steve Allen as he mentored me through critical seasons of my journey as a worshiper, father, husband, friend, and entrepreneur. I am extremely thankful for this book. It is a treasure trove of wisdom and revelation for anyone seeking to make an impact and take their mountain!

Traylor Woodall
CEO Fivestone Studios

And He Ran for 40 Days is a bold, transformative and entirely unique account of two men's journeys. With a biblical basis of change, this book will provide the platform to initiate major developments in one's life while simultaneously pointing the reader back to an appreciation for today through an irresistible focus on God's call on your life. The journey of Elijah is biblical, explained, and empowering while Steve's journey is raw, authentic, and inspirational; both are masterfully woven into this thought-provoking call to faith and action.

Scott Wright
Believer and Professional Engineer

A WORD OF ENCOURAGEMENT TO ALL THOSE WHO PRESENTLY ARE IN THE FIERY CRUCIBLE OF TESTING

But he knows the way that I take;
when he has tested me, I will come forth as gold.
My feet have closely followed his steps;
I have kept to his way without turning aside.
I have not departed from the commands of his lips;
I have treasured the words of his mouth more than my daily bread.

Job 23:10-12 (NIV)

WALK WITH ME

GOD'S SOLUTIONS FOR
AMERICA'S
HURTING
CHILDREN

BY SAMANTHA ALLEN AND SARAH WEBB

WALK WITH ME

THE POPULATION OF CHILDREN IN FOSTER CARE IN AMERICA THAT NEEDS GODLY FAMILIES CONTINUES TO GROW. WHEN ABORTION IS OVERTURNED, WHO WILL WANT ALL THE BABIES? GOD'S HEART LONGS FOR THEM, AND HE HAS THE ANSWERS TO MAKE A WAY FOR THEM. WHILE SHARING PERSONAL EXPERIENCES FROM HER FAMILY'S ADOPTION, SAMANTHA PRESENTS A PRAYER STRATEGY TO MARSHAL HEAVEN'S RESOURCES AND ENCOURAGE THE AMERICAN CHURCH TO INSERT HERSELF IN TO THE STORY OF GOD'S WAITING CHILDREN. SARAH SHARES A POWERFUL PRAYER MANUAL THAT WILL CATALYZE THE PEOPLE OF GOD TO PRAY THIS ASSIGNMENT TO COMPLETION!

"READ THIS BOOK AND THEN LET THE PEN OF GOD REWRITE THE STORIES OF THE MOST NEGLECTED AND INNOCENT ONES THROUGH YOU!"
LOU ENGLE, LOU ENGLE MINISTRIES

"WE HAVE NOT ONLY KNOWN SAMANTHA AND STEVE FOR OVER THREE DECADES, BUT WE HAVE HAD THE PRIVILEGE OF WATCHING THEM LIVE OUT THE CALL OF THE FATHER IN SO MANY AREAS OF OUR EXISTENCE, INCLUDING THE CALL TO GIVE A HOME TO THE ORPHAN. THERE ARE NOT MANY COUPLES WHO HAVE THE AUTHORITY TO GIVE THIS CHARGE TO THE CHURCH, BUT SAMANTHA AND STEVE DO. WE ARE EXCITED THAT IN THIS BOOK THEY HAVE SHARED THEIR STORY AND, MORE IMPORTANTLY, OUR HEAVENLY FATHER'S HEART FOR THE ORPHAN. IT IS OUR PRAYER THAT THE CHURCH WILL HAVE GRACE TO BE A TOOL THROUGH WHICH THE FATHER CAN PLACE EVERY ORPHAN INTO A FAMILY. (PSALM 68:6)"
DAVID AND JEANNETTE MCQUEEN, ADOPTIVE PARENTS
LEAD PASTORS AT BELTWAY PARK CHURCH, ABILENE, TEXAS

"'WALK WITH ME' IS AN INVITATION IN TO THE FATHER HEART OF GOD FOR THE FATHERLESS AND ORPHAN. YOU WILL NOT BE THE SAME PERSON BY THE TIME YOU FINISH READING IT! SAMANTHA'S JOURNEY WITH HER FAMILY DISPLAYS JAMES 1:27 TRUE RELIGION OUT OF RELATIONSHIP WITH GOD. I BELIEVE WITH ALL MY HEART THAT THERE ARE PLACES IN GOD'S HEART THAT WE WILL NEVER GET TO EXPERIENCE IF WE DO NOT SAY "YES" TO HIS HEART FOR ADOPTION, HOWEVER THAT LOOKS FOR EACH ONE OF US."
DANIELLE HELMER
REGIONAL CONFERENCE COORDINATOR, CONTEND GLOBAL

"'WALK WITH ME' IS A BOOK THAT REVEALS THE TENDER HEART OF GOD TOWARD ALL OF HIS CHILDREN AND INVITES YOU TO OPEN YOUR'S."
JEFF DOLLAR, SENIOR PASTOR, GRACE CENTER, FRANKLIN, TENNESSEE

ALLEN FAMILY MINISTRIES

WALK WITH ME
COPYRIGHT © 2019 BY SAMANTHA ALLEN

SAMANTHA ALLEN
SUPPORT@ALLENFAMILYMINISTRIES.ORG
HTTPS://ALLENFAMILYMINISTRIES.ORG/

$15.95
ISBN 978-1-7338107-0-8
51595>
9 781733 810708

STEVE ALLEN

EXPLORING THE LIFE OF JOSEPH AND THE TRANSFORMATIVE
POWER OF *LIVING A LIFE OF KINGDOM VISION*

THE

VISION

JOURNEY

SEVEN STRATEGIC KEYS THAT
UNLOCKED THE DESTINY OF JOSEPH

COMING IN 2020

HOW IS YOUR VISION?

The Vision Journey is an invitation to learn from the life of one of the most known and loved biblical patriarchs, Joseph. Given an epic dream that foretold his future at the age of 17, Joseph then endured 13 years of desert training before ascending to the throne in the palaces of Egypt. Come join me as we walk with Joseph during those desert years, in which he learns from Father God the ways of the King and His Kingdom.

We will learn why character is 10 times more important than competencies in the economy of God, as we nevertheless strive to grow in excellence. We will also study why vision is so important for the man and woman of God in this generation. Too, we will work to craft a transformative personal vision statement for our lives, for the days that we are walking in and for the future tumultuous seasons that are quickly approaching.

My personal testimony is that I've been decreeing daily my vision statement out loud for the past 10 years and it has changed my life. You become what you behold. As you seek His face, as you pursue the One who has pursued you, you are transformed into His very nature!

Steve Allen
November 22, 2019
In the shadow of the Rockies
Colorado Springs, Colorado USA

STEVE'S VISION STATEMENT

I am called to be a father who walks in passion, purity, power, and perseverance in the Lord. I seek to know and love Yeshua with all my heart, soul, mind and strength and make Him known. I delight to love, cherish and champion my Proverbs 31 wife and father sons and daughters who will change the world because they are following in the steps of THE WORLD CHANGER! As an Abraham, I will climb my mountain, overcome giants and receive my full inheritance as a father. I will not die but live and tell what the Lord has done!

The Living Word of God is a sword in my hands, a fire in my heart, and truth upon my tongue. I will pray it. Live it. And proclaim it; Until the Desired of the Nations returns!

I am called to be a watchman on the walls of Israel and in the Spirit, cry out for her salvation day and night, until a mighty river of revival flows through the earth.

As a Leadership Coach, I will help others break through their barriers, overcome their obstacles to take hold of their destinies. I will wholeheartedly seek to make others great as I help empower and propel them in their God-given assignments!

My Mission... is to raise up 10,000 sons who become 10,000 God-fearing, God-loving fathers who disciple nations in preparation for the return of the King!

And finally... I will lay down my life for the One who has laid down His life for me.